LEGENDS OF WARFARE
GROUND

German Light Armored Cars of WWII

Sd.Kfz. 221, 222, 223, 247, 260, and 261

DAVID DOYLE

Schiffer
Military History
4880 Lower Valley Road
Atglen, PA 19310

Other Schiffer books by the author

German Heavy Armored Cars: Sd.Kfz. 231, 232, 233, 263, and 234 in World War II,
978-0-7643-6649-9

Hummel and Nashorn/Hornisse: German Self-Propelled Artillery in World War II,
978-0-7643-5940-8

Panzerkampfwagen IV: The Backbone of Germany's WWII Tank Forces,
978-0-7643-5359-8

Library of Congress Control Number: 2026933018

Designed by Alexa Harris
Type set in Impact / Univers Lt STD / Minion Pro

ISBN: 978-0-7643-7158-5
ePub: 978-1-5073-0720-5
Printed in India
10 9 8 7 6 5 4 3 2 1

MIX
Paper | Supporting responsible forestry
FSC™ C016779

Published by Schiffer Publishing, Ltd.
4880 Lower Valley Road
Atglen, PA 19310
Phone: (610) 593-1777; Fax: (610) 593-2002
Email: Info@schifferbooks.com
Web: www.schifferbooks.com

Acknowledgments

This book would not have been possible without the generous assistance of many individuals and organizations. In particular, I would like to thank Tom Kailbourn, Thomas Anderson, David Fletcher and the Tank Museum, Holger Erdmann and Detlev Terlisten of Nuts & Bolts, the late Stefan DeMeyer, Tom Laemlein, Pat Ware, Chris Hughes, Scott Taylor, and the staffs of the Patton Museum, National Archives, and Military History Institute. All wartime photos not otherwise credited are from the US National Archives; all post–World War II photos not otherwise credited are by the author.

Of course, none of this would have materialized without the ongoing help and support of my wife, Denise, who not only endures long hours in musty archives but always provides encouragement and inspiration.

Contents

Introduction

The Treaty of Versailles, which formally ended the First World War, explicitly forbade Germany from possessing, manufacturing, or acquiring armored vehicles. Specifically addressing armored cars, Article 171 of the treaty stated: "The manufacture and the importation into Germany of armored cars, tanks and all similar constructions suitable for use in war are also prohibited."

Despite these restrictions, domestic political instability in Germany led to an amendment to the Treaty of Versailles. This modification, formalized by the Supreme Council at Boulogne in June 1920, permitted Germany to maintain a limited number of on-road armored vehicles strictly for internal-policing purposes.

As Hitler came to power in 1933, Germany accelerated its covert rearmament program. The German military leadership had never fully accepted the Versailles restrictions and had maintained relationships with Soviet Russia, where German tank designs were secretly tested throughout the 1920s. By 1935, Hitler openly renounced the military restrictions of Versailles, and German armored-vehicle development continued to proceed without pretense.

Early Armored Cars: Kfz 13 and Kfz 14

By 1932, Germany began producing two types of armored cars that were no longer disguised as police vehicles: the *Maschinengewehrkraftwagen* (Kfz 13) and the *Funkkraftwagen* (Kfz 14). Both utilized reinforced civilian Daimler-Benz and Adler automobile chassis, which proved inadequate for military applications.

Regardless of the underlying chassis manufacturer, these vehicles shared similar appearances. Daimler-Benz handled the conversion process for its own chassis as well as those from Adler, mounting armored bodies onto the platforms. The thin armor plating could withstand only standard 7.92 mm ammunition, with armor-piercing protection limited to the vehicle's front section.

The *Maschinengewehrkraftwagen* Kfz 13, as its name suggests, featured a pedestal-mounted 7.92 mm MG 13 machine gun with 360-degree rotation capability. Each vehicle carried a thousand rounds of ammunition.

In contrast, the *Funkkraftwagen* Kfz 14 omitted the machine gun, instead utilizing the interior space for a 5-watt communication system capable of both voice and Morse code transmission.

Between 1933 and 1935, production totaled 30 radio vehicles and 116 machine gun carriers. When Germany invaded Poland in September 1939, these early vehicles were largely relegated to training duties. According to Bundesarchiv records, a few saw limited action with reserve units during the French campaign of 1940, but their thin armor and limited off-road mobility proved significant handicaps against even light antitank weapons.

The *Maschinengewehrkraftwagen* (Kfz. 13) was a simple armored car built on a commercial car chassis and equipped with 8 mm steel plate. Designed for the interwar Reichwehr, they were intended to provide basic training to motorized troops. Armament was the MG 13 7.92 mm machine gun, mounted on a pedestal and protected by an armored shield also of 8 mm thickness. There was a radio-equipped version known as the *Funkkraftwagen* (Kfz. 14).

CHAPTER 1

Sd.Kfz. 221: The First Purpose-Built Light Armored Car

Unlike its predecessors, the Sonderkraftfahrzeug Sd.Kfz. 221 utilized a purpose-built chassis designed specifically for armored vehicles by Auto-Union's Horch division. This fundamental difference explains the designation change from simple *Kraftfahrzeug* (vehicle) to *Sonderkraftfahrzeug* (specialized vehicle). The initial prototype chassis was completed in July 1934. Following approval, Horch commenced series production of the chassis, designated Typ 801. The armored bodies for the Sd.Kfz. 221 were manufactured by three firms: Deutsche Edelstahlwerke in Hannover, Boehler-Werke in Kapfenberg, and Schoeller-Bleckmann in Mürzzuschlag.

The Sd.Kfz. 221 offered significant improvements in mobility, with four-wheel drive and four-wheel steering combined with a relatively powerful engine for its era, providing acceptable performance both on- and off-road.

The vehicle featured a manually rotated open-topped gun shield on its roof that resembled a turret at first glance. Folding screens provided additional protection against hand grenades being thrown into the fighting compartment behind this shield. A single vision port ahead of the driver provided visibility—a notable difference from the Sd.Kfz. 222 and other vehicles in the family, which were equipped with two vision ports in the front of the superstructure.

Initial Sd.Kfz. 221 production spanned three manufacturing lots or series corresponding to different contracts. The chassis (*fahrgestell*) numbers for these groups were 810001–810359, 810360–810485, and 810486–810635. It's worth noting that these represent chassis numbers, and some within each range were allocated to other armored-car variants.

Sd.Kfz. 221 Series Development and Variations

Series 1 (1935–1937)

The initial production run of the Sd.Kfz. 221 began in 1935, following the completion and approval of the prototype chassis in July 1934. These first vehicles utilized the Horch Typ 801 chassis with chassis numbers within the 810001–810359 range, though not all chassis in this range were used for the Sd.Kfz. 221. Assembly

This trial version of the Sd.Kfz. 221, likely photographed in 1935, had a body similar in design to that of the production Sd.Kfz. 221, with noticeable differences including a different rotating gun shield design, a pedestal for a 7.92 mm MG 13 above the front of the gun shield, and a raised top for the driver's compartment that was noticeably higher than that of the production Sd.Kfz. 221. *Holger Erdmann via Detlev Terlisten / Nuts & Bolts*

A first-series Sd.Kfz. 221, license number WH-27140, appears to have become mired next to an embankment. Early-production Sd.Kfz. 221s had small cutouts on the front fenders to provide clearance for the service headlights. Rain gutters were fitted over the driver's visors. The rods with white balls on the ends on the front fenders helped the driver gauge the clearance with objects to the sides. *Holger Erdmann via Detlev Terlisten / Nuts & Bolts*

was divided among several manufacturers, with Daimler-Benz producing fourteen, and shipbuilders Deutsche-Werke (Kiel), and Schichau (Elbing) completing sixty and sixty-nine, respectively. These vehicles featured the original 75 hp Horch V-8 engine, which provided adequate but not exceptional mobility. The primary armament consisted of the MG 13 machine gun mounted in the distinctive manually rotated open-topped gun shield on the roof. The folding screens for grenade protection were already present in this initial series. These vehicles represented the first purpose-built German armored cars of the prewar period and established the basic configuration that would continue throughout production.

Visually, all three series of the Sd.Kfz. 221 feature Reuleaux triangle bolt-on *Radpanzer* (armor for wheel hubs). The first series vehicles have a flagstaff on the left front fender, and the turn signals are mounted on the sides of the body. The visors in the hull and turret were made of flat plate.

Series 2 (April–November 1938)

The second production batch is known to consist of forty-six vehicles, using chassis numbers from the 810360–810485 range. There is some evidence that eight further vehicles of this series were produced for the SS. The second-series vehicles continued to use the Horch Typ 801 chassis and maintained the same basic mechanical configuration as the first series. A significant change occurred after March 10, 1938, when a military directive ordered the replacement of the MG 13 with the improved MG 34 machine gun. This transition may have happened during this production series, with later vehicles receiving the newer machine gun directly from the factory. The overall hull design, armor protection, and mobility characteristics remained consistent with the first series. These vehicles continued to receive the 75 hp engine and featured the same four-wheel-drive and four-wheel-steering capabilities that characterized the design.

Externally, the steel guards now protected the turn signals.

Series 3 (June 1939–August 1940)

The third series utilized chassis numbers from the 810486–810635 range. By this time, all new vehicles were equipped with the MG 34 machine gun as standard armament. On the basis of early field experience, minor improvements may have been made to the interior layout and stowage arrangements, but the fundamental design remained unchanged. Assembled by Weserhütte, Bad Oeynhausen, the Horch Typ 801 chassis, with its 75 hp engine, continued to serve as the basis for these vehicles. By this point,

On the production Sd.Kfz. 221s, as seen in this photo of a first-series vehicle, the roof of the driver's compartment was slightly higher than the deck to the rear of it. During production of the first-series Sd.Kfz. 221s, the front fenders were redesigned, with a sweeping curve on the bottoms, as seen here. No cutouts for the headlights were necessary with these fenders.

Civilians crowd around a first-series Sd.Kfz. 221. A characteristic of the early Sd.Kfz. 221s was the use of triangular hinges on the top and rear engine-access doors; by the time of the third series of these vehicles, these hinges were changed to rectangular ones. Rubber mud flaps were mounted on the bottoms of the rear fenders. The right muffler is to the side of the fender.

users were beginning to note the limitations of the design, particularly regarding the power-to-weight ratio, since crews often carried additional equipment beyond the vehicle's original design specifications. In fact, the operator's manual explicitly warned that vehicles were loaded to their maximum capacity with standard equipment.

Third-series vehicles can be distinguished from their predecessors as a result of cast-armor vision slits and ports, rather than the previously used flat plate. The roof over the driver was raised compared to earlier models, providing additional headroom. The hinges for the motor hatch were now armored and no longer were of a triangular shape. A flagstaff no longer was mounted on the left front fender, but a 35-watt Notek blackout driving light was.

Field Modifications (1940–1942)

Though not a distinct production series, many existing Sd.Kfz. 221 vehicles underwent field modifications during their service life. The most significant was the retrofitting of the 2.8 cm *schwere Panzerbüchse* 41 to selected vehicles, improving their anti-armor capabilities. Other common field modifications included additional external stowage, improved radio equipment when vehicles operated alongside Sd.Kfz. 223 radio cars, and various winterization measures for operations on the eastern front. Since production of the Sd.Kfz. 221 had ceased in August 1940 after a total of 339 vehicles, no factory-new vehicles incorporating these lessons were produced.

Throughout all series, the Sd.Kfz. 221 maintained its characteristic basic design: a small, light armored car with four-wheel drive and four-wheel steering, thin armor protection sufficient only against small-arms fire, and the distinctive open-topped gun shield that gave it the appearance of having a small turret. As the war progressed, these vehicles were increasingly relegated to secondary theaters and training duties as their limitations became more apparent in the face of improving enemy antitank capabilities and the challenging terrain of the eastern front.

Field Use

The Sd.Kfz. 221 was extensively used during the Polish campaign of 1939, where the vehicles performed adequately on the good road network of Poland. However, according to war diaries of the 3rd Panzer Division's reconnaissance battalion, even in Poland, crews reported concerns about the vehicle's thin armor. During the invasion of France in 1940, these vehicles operated effectively as reconnaissance platforms but proved vulnerable to French antitank rifles.

The ultimate test came during Operation Barbarossa in 1941. The Russian steppe, with its vast distances, poor roads, and harsh weather, exposed the limitations of these light vehicles. War diaries from multiple *Aufklärungs-Abteilungen* (reconnaissance battalions) note that many Sd.Kfz. 221s broke down during extended operations in the mud and snow. Their thin armor provided little protection against Soviet 14.5 mm antitank rifles. By mid-1942, surviving vehicles were primarily allocated to occupation duties in western Europe or for training.

Production ceased in August 1940, after 339 Sd.Kfz. 221 units had been manufactured.

A series 1 Sd.Kfz. 221, license number WH 479064, is driving up a concrete ramp along the English Channel in France in June 1940. Above the gun shield, two hinged screens for deflecting hand grenades, called *Gitterklappen*, are secured in their open positions. The open grille to the rear of the gun shield, the *Schutzgitter*, protected the fighting compartment from tossed grenades when closed. When open, it was possible to seat a passenger in the rear of the fighting compartment. On the left front fender, in addition to the clearance guide and rearview mirror, are a flagstaff for holding a pennant, and a Notek blackout headlight.

An Sd.Kfz. 221 is standing by in an unidentified village. Mounted with three screws on each wheel is a *Radpanzer*, a piece of armor to protect the wheel hub. These items were triangular in shape with rounded corners. The vehicle commander/gunner's helmet is visible above the gun shield.

Parked next to an Sd.Kfz. 232 *Panzerfunkwagen* during a road march is a first-series Sd.Kfz. 221. The letter "G" on the vehicles indicates that they were part of Panzer Group Guderian (redesignated 2nd Panzer Group in November 1940 and 2nd Panzer Army in October 1941). A storage box is secured above the bumper of the Sd.Kfz. 221, and a Notek blackout headlight, turned to the rear, is on the left fender.

A first-series Sd.Kfz. 221 is part of a column of vehicles advancing through a town in Poland during the 1939 invasion of that country. The solid white *Balkenkreuz* (cross) was used on Wehrmacht vehicles specifically in the invasion of Poland. The driver's front visor is secured open in an upright position, and a detachable windshield with two small wipers has been installed in the opening.

A bundle of sticks is tied to the front of this Sd.Kfz. 221; these were used for bridging over trenches and deep mud. Fabric covers with blackout slits are fitted over the headlight lenses. A unit crest is on the left fender, while the tactical sign for a reconnaissance company is on the right fender.

A column of light armored cars, including a first-series Sd.Kfz. 221 in the foreground, is passing through a war-torn village. The license plate number is WH 119348 or 119349. Painted on the armored body above the right rear fender is what appears to be "ARRAS," a reference to a battle and German victory in France on May 21, 1940. A spare tire with a cover is stored on the right side of the body.

This first-series Sd.Kfz. 221 has been retrofitted with a frame antenna and radio equipment, no doubt resulting in a very cramped interior. On the right front fender, a good-luck horseshoe has been mounted.

The second-series Sd.Kfz. 221 composed a small batch of forty-six vehicles completed between April and November 1938. One source speculates that an additional eight vehicles were completed under this series for the Waffen-SS, such as this Sd.Kfz. 221, which bears an SS license plate numbered 4780. A noticeable new feature with this series was the addition of two more vision slits to the gun shield; like the driver's visors and the two original gun shield vision slits, the new vision slits were fabricated from flat armor plates. The new vision slit on the left side of the gun shield is the higher one, under the vehicle commander's elbow. *Holger Erdmann via Detlev Terlisten / Nuts & Bolts*

A second-series Sd.Kfz. 221 photographed in a war-ravaged village has much equipment and baggage aboard, including a tarpaulin, a tow cable, and two unrecognizable box-shaped objects on the front and bedrolls on the sides of the body.

A German soldier, *left*, and a group of boys are looking at a third-series Sd.Kfz. 221, license number WH 210454, with the side engine compartment doors propped open. A key feature of the series 3 cars was the replacement of the original driver's visors and the gun shield vision slits with new ones formed of cast armor. This was one of a number of Sd.Kfz. 221s armed, in addition to the standard 7.92 mm MG 34, with a 7.9 mm *Panzerabwehrbüchse* 39 (PzB 39) antitank rifle, mounted in the right side of the gun shield.

A third-series Sd.Kfz. 221 is crossing a makeshift wooden bridge over a ditch while motorcyclists stand by in the background. The bottom plate of the bow has been battered. Storage boxes are secured to the bow and the right front fender, while a jerry can is in a holder toward the rear of the armored body.

During the German invasion of Greece in 1941, a third-series Sd.Kfz. 221 from *Panzeraufklärungs-Abteilung* 8 (Panzer Reconnaissance Battalion 8), of the 5th Panzer Division, is parked at the base of the Acropolis, in Athens. The cast-armor vision slits on the gun shield are seen to good advantage, with their pronounced bulges that were thicker at the top than the bottom. A brush guard is around the left turn signal, to the rear of the driver's side visor; this feature was introduced during second-series production.

A third-series Sd.Kfz. 221 is pulling away from a curb in an unidentified city. The license plate, unusually located on the left fender instead of the bow, is partly hidden but shows the number: 13511. Faintly visible on the front of the armored body is a pennant-shaped tactical symbol with the number 2 below it. On the third-series vehicles, the flagstaff on the left fender was discontinued.

Troops are marching past a third-series Sd.Kfz. 221. The side doors of the engine compartment have been opened, likely to facilitate cooling of the compartment. A large coil of wire is secured to the engine deck. On the vision slits on the gun shield, the actual slits are near the bottoms of the castings and are visible only under high magnification.

Two jerry cans are tied to the front of this third-series Sd.Kfz. 221, and a Notek blackout headlight is on the left front fender. A dustcover is secured over the barrel of the MG 34, and a dust-covered *Balkenkreuz*, black with white borders, is faintly visible above the storage box at the center of the armored boy. A shovel is secured to brackets on the side of the body.

A destroyed third-series Sd.Kfz. 221 is observed from the left rear. This example has the cast-armor visors, triangular wheel armor, and armored hinges for the engine-compartment doors. On the rear of the armored body is the tactical sign for a reconnaissance company.

The crewman of a third-series Sd.Kfz. 221 stands lookout atop the vehicle as the other crewman climbs aboard. Whitewash has been brushed over the original gray paint for winter camouflage. Toward the top of the box secured above the front bumper is part of a tactical sign for a reconnaissance company. The vehicle is armed with an MG 34 and a PzB 39 antitank rifle.

During 1942, a quantity of Sd.Kfz. 221s were converted to carriers for the 2.8 cm 2.8 *schwere Panzerbüchse* 41 (sPzB 41) antitank rifle. The weapon was installed on a mount on the roof of the driver's compartment. To provide clearance for traversing the gun, the front of the gun shield armor was cut out. This example of the zPzB 41–armed Sd.Kfz. 221 was based on a second-series vehicle. *Holger Erdmann via Detlev Terlisten / Nuts & Bolts*

While small by antitank gun standards, the *schwere Panzerbüchse* 41 was, in fact, a large rifle. It was originally to be mounted on a single axle but could also be mounted on the ammunition trailer of the JF 8 infantry lumber. Just the barrel and muzzle brake together weighed nearly 100 pounds, making some sort of mount necessary. *Walter J. Spielberger collection*

Rheinmetall, the manufacturer of the *schwere Panzerbüchse* 41, took this photo of the antitank rifle on an experimental carriage in March 1940. The principle behind the *schwere Panzerbüchse* 41, and all taperbore weapons, is to increase the velocity of the projectile. *Walter J. Spielberger collection*

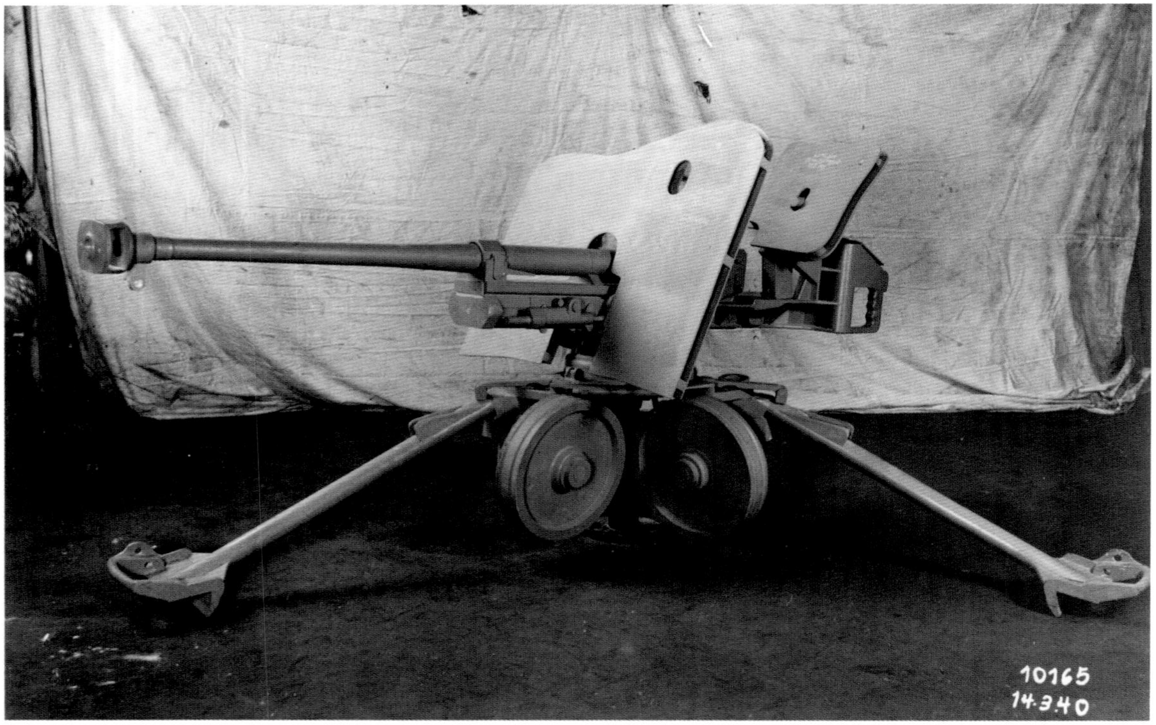

The effectiveness of increased velocity can be illustrated through this simple example. Were a rifle bullet to be dropped on someone's leg, it would scarcely be noticed. If it were launched at the same leg using a child's slingshot, it would be felt, and perhaps a bruise would be left. Were it to be fired by a rifle, a wound would surely result. The rifle bullet has remained the same in each case, but the velocity has been increased incrementally. *Walter J. Spielberger collection*

It is not believed that the heavy antitank rifle was fielded using the experimental, tripod carriage shown here. One of the shortcomings of the weapon is the requirement for tungsten in the projectile. Lesser metals would simply shatter on impact with armor at the velocities achieved by the *schwere Panzerbüchse* 41, but tungsten was also required for machine tool production, and Germany had precious little of the metal. *Walter J. Spielberger collection*

As seen in this overhead view, the muzzle brake of the *schwere Panzerbüchse* 41 was quite stubby. While by midwar, armor had improved to the point that the *schwere Panzerbüchse* 41 was no longer an ineffective antitank weapon, it remained effective against lesser-armored vehicles, and light fortifications. *Walter J. Spielberger collection*

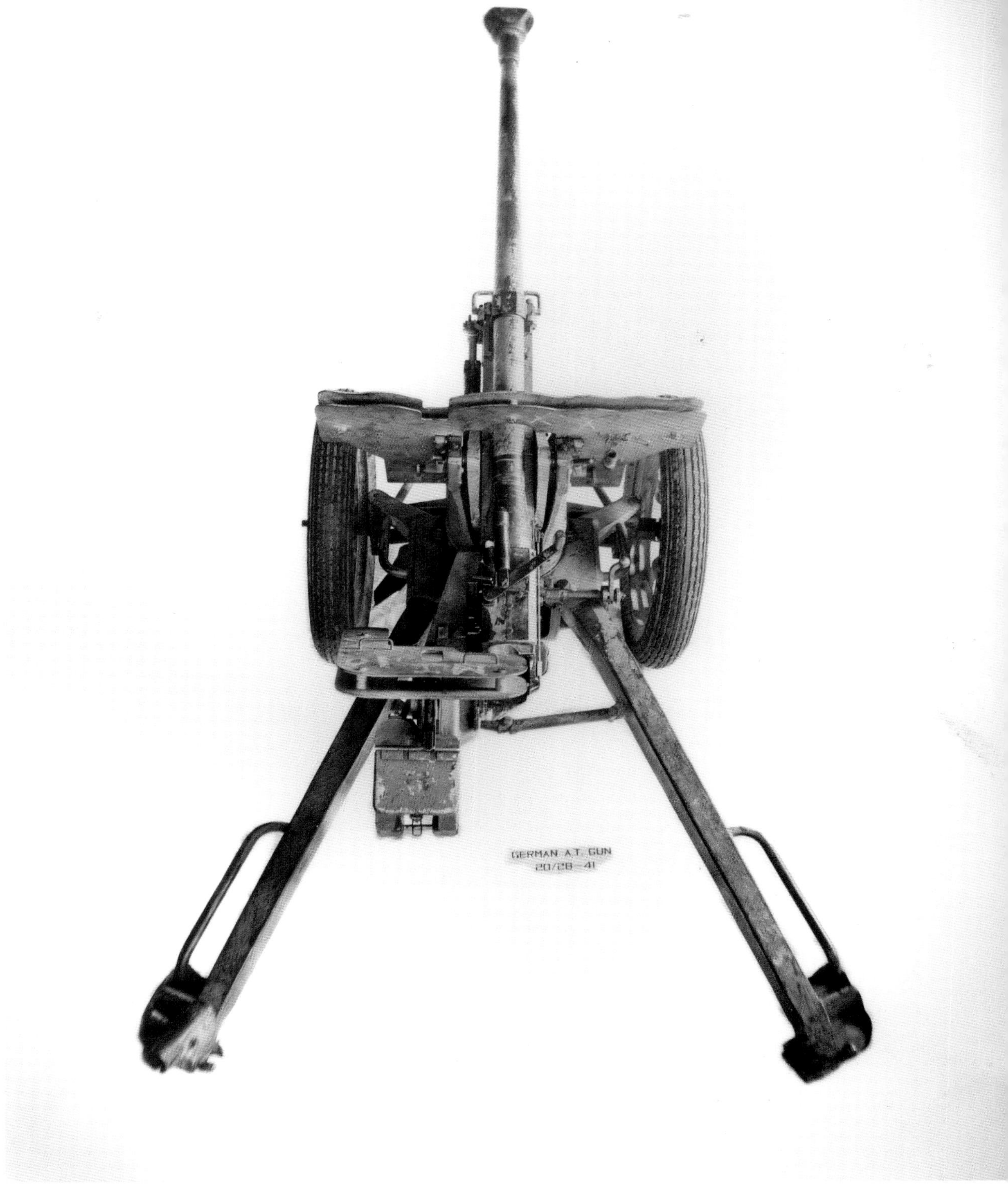

This Sd.Kfz. 221 with 2.8 cm sPzB 41 was converted from a third-series vehicle, with cast-armor driver's visors. The zPzB 41 operated on the squeeze-bore principle. The bore of the barrel was tapered from 2.8 cm at the gun chamber to 2 cm at the muzzle. This caused the pressure of the propellant gases to be high as the projectile exited the barrel, resulting in a very high muzzle velocity, 4,500 feet per second, with attending increased penetrating power. The gun's shields, consisting of a large unit in the front and a smaller one to the front of the gunner's face, were made of two thin sheets of armor with a space between them.

A third-series Sd.Kfz. 221 is armed with a 2.8 cm sPzB 41. The projectile fired by this rifle had a tungsten core, which provided excellent armor-piercing qualities. The gunner aimed the piece manually, like a machine gun.

CHAPTER 2

Sd.Kfz. 222: The Standard Light Armored Car

The Sd.Kfz. 222 shared the Horch Typ 801 (and later Typ 801v) chassis with the Sd.Kfz. 221 but featured substantially different armament: a 2 cm KwK 38 cannon with a coaxial MG 34 machine gun in its turret. This significant firepower upgrade made the Sd.Kfz. 222 the mainstay of German reconnaissance forces throughout the war.

Like its siblings, the Sd.Kfz. 222 initially utilized the Horch Typ 801 chassis with four-wheel drive and four-wheel steering. Though these features provided satisfactory off-road capability, drivers received explicit instructions that vehicles should operate on-road whenever possible. Four-wheel steering was to be engaged only during off-road travel or slow-speed maneuvers in confined spaces. Safety concerns led to strict prohibition against using four-wheel steering at highway speeds.

A three-man crew consisting of driver, loader, and commander/gunner operated the Sd.Kfz. 222.

Total production reached 990 Sd.Kfz. 222 vehicles across five manufacturing groups (series). The first four groups composed the Ausf. A variant, while the final group represented the Ausf. B model. Beginning in 1941 and continuing until the end of production, radio equipment was installed in new Sd.Kfz. 222 vehicles. Similar upgrades were intended for retrofitting to earlier production models.

Series 1 (1935–1937)

The initial production of the Sd.Kfz. 222 began in 1935, with a total of seventy-two vehicles manufactured through 1937. These vehicles were distributed among three manufacturers: Daimler-Benz produced ten units, Schichau assembled thirty-six, and Deutches-Werke manufactured twenty-six. These early models utilized the Horch Typ 801 chassis in the 810001–810359 range, featuring four-wheel drive and four-wheel steering. The most distinctive feature of the Sd.Kfz. 222 compared to the Sd.Kfz. 221 was its armament: a 2 cm automatic cannon and a coaxial machine gun. The first series was equipped with the earlier model of the 2 cm cannon and the MG 13 machine gun. The vehicles featured an open-topped turret with mesh antigrenade screens that could be folded when not needed. These early vehicles did not come with radio equipment as standard. The crew consisted of three men: driver, gunner, and commander/loader, allowing for more efficient operation of the dual weapon system compared to the two-man crew of the Sd.Kfz. 221.

The first-series vehicles have a flagstaff on the left front fender and turn signals mounted on the sides of the body. The visors in the hull and turret were made of flat plate.

Series 2 (April–November 1938)

The second production series comprised seventy-two vehicles built between April and November 1938. These vehicles were assembled on chassis in the serial number 810360–810485 range. These vehicles maintained the same basic configuration as the first series but incorporated lessons learned from early operational use. The most significant change implemented during this production run was the transition from the MG 13 to the improved MG 34 machine gun, following the March 10, 1938, directive. This change provided increased firepower with the more reliable and higher-rate-of-fire MG 34. The Horch Typ 801 chassis remained unchanged, with its 75 hp engine, four-wheel drive, and four-wheel steering. The turret design and 2 cm main armament remained consistent with the first series. As with the earlier vehicles, radio equipment was not standard.

Beginning with the second series, protective frames were installed around the turn signals.

Series 3 (June 1939–January 1940)

The third production batch was smaller, consisting of only sixty-four vehicles assembled by Schichau between June 1939 and January 1940. By this time, the MG 34 was firmly established as the standard coaxial machine gun. These vehicles continued to utilize the Horch Typ 801 chassis in the serial number 810636–810699 range, with the 75 hp engine. Minor refinements may have been incorporated on the basis of feedback from units that had operated the vehicles during the annexation of Austria, the occupation of Czechoslovakia, and the early stages of the Polish campaign. However, the fundamental design remained consistent with earlier production vehicles. No significant changes to armor protection were made, although cast-armor vision slits and ports, rather than the previously used flat plate, were used and armored hinges were used to secure the motor hatches. A flagstaff no longer was mounted on the left front fender, but a 35-watt Notek blackout driving light was.

Series 4 (September 1940–December 1941)

The fourth and largest Ausf. A production series comprised 232 vehicles manufactured by Schichau from September 1940 through December 1941. This series introduced more-substantial changes based on combat experience from the Polish and French campaigns. The most significant upgrade was the implementation of the improved mounting for the 2 cm KwK 38 cannon, which had improved steering and elevation controls and increased maximum elevation from 80 to 85 degrees. These changes enhanced the vehicle's capability against aircraft and targets in elevated positions and also required high screens to be installed over the turret. While still built on the Horch Typ 801 chassis (serial numbers 810818–81014140), these vehicles likely incorporated various minor mechanical improvements on the basis of field experience. Beginning in 1941, radio equipment was installed as standard in new production vehicles, significantly enhancing their operational utility for reconnaissance missions. This communication capability had previously been limited to the specialized Sd.Kfz. 223 variant.

The Reuleaux triangle bolt-on *Radpanzer* (armor for wheel hubs) used on previous models was replaced by disc-shaped hub armor.

Series 5 / Ausf. B (May 1942–June 1943)

The final production series represented the most comprehensive upgrade of the Sd.Kfz. 222 and was designated as the Ausf. B variant. A total of 550 vehicles were produced between May 1942 and June 1943, with 350 completed at the Büssing-NAG facility and 200 at Schichau. The most substantial improvement was the implementation of the upgraded Horch Typ 801v chassis, serial numbers 8110004–8110994. This chassis featured a more powerful

The Sd.Kfz. 222 had an armored body similar in shape to that of the Sd.Kfz. 221. The turret of the Sd.Kfz. 222 was larger, to accommodate a 2 cm KwK 30 automatic gun and a 7.92 mm MG 13 (replaced later with a 7.92 mm MG 34). The *Gitterklappen* antigrenade screens on the turret were taller than those of the Sd.Kfz. 221, having vertical panels on the front and sides that acted to extend the height of the screens.

This first-series Sd.Kfz. 222 exhibits the defining characteristics of the series: flagstaff on left front fender, unguarded turn signal arms on the hull side, flat plate visors, and Reuleaux triangle-shaped bolt-on armor for the wheel hubs. This 1. Panzer Division vehicle was photographed just prior to the launch of Barbarossa. *Holger Erdmann via Detlev Terlisten / Nuts & Bolts*

90 hp engine, improved transmission, enhanced shock absorbers, and power brakes. These mechanical upgrades significantly improved the vehicle's mobility and reliability, particularly in challenging terrain.

Also changed was the armored body, which previously was divided into two sections, was now of a standardized type consisting of three sections, and was used across multiple light armored car types. The series 5 continued to use the 2 cm KwK 38 cannon and MG 34 machine gun, though the turret no longer had side vision ports. Radio equipment was standard in all Ausf. B vehicles. Additional improvements based on eastern front experience may have included enhanced winterization features, improved ventilation, and refined internal layout for better crew ergonomics.

With the introduction of the fifth series, the turn signals were relocated from the sides of the armored body to the front fenders.

Field Use

The Sd.Kfz. 222 saw action on all fronts throughout the war. In Poland and France, its mobility and firepower proved highly effective for reconnaissance and screening operations. However, during the North African campaign, the vehicle's enclosed turret design with limited ventilation caused severe discomfort for crews in desert heat, but the vehicles remained operational throughout the campaign with Rommel's forces.

In Russia the Sd.Kfz. 222 initially performed well, but as with the Sd.Kfz. 221, the harsh conditions and vast distances strained maintenance capabilities. The 20 mm cannon proved effective against Soviet light vehicles and infantry but was inadequate against T-34 tanks.

Throughout their service life, many Sd.Kfz. 222 vehicles underwent field modifications to address operational requirements. Common modifications included additional external stowage for extended operations, enhanced radio equipment, and various winterization measures for eastern front operations. Some units added impromptu armor reinforcement, though this often negatively impacted mobility due to the additional weight. The open-mesh antigrenade screens were sometimes reinforced or modified on the basis of field experience.

By 1943, increasing Allied air superiority made daylight reconnaissance missions hazardous. Unit reports from the eastern front indicate that many Sd.Kfz. 222 vehicles were relegated to night operations to avoid air attack. Despite these challenges, the vehicle remained in frontline service until the war's end, with some units fighting in the Battle of Berlin in 1945.

The *Leichte Panzerspähwagen* Sd.Kfz. 222 (2 cm) was intended to provide armed might for the reconnaissance arm. This series 1 vehicle has been retrofitted with a Notek blackout driving light.

Photographed during a road march was a first-series Sd.Kfz. 222, followed by an Sd.Kfz. 223 (FU) and an Sd.Kfz. 221. Mounted on the rear of the right front fender of the Sd.Kfz. 221 is a storage box of apparently nonstandard design; it is wedge shaped, so that the top of the box runs parallel with the top of the fender.

Snow chains are installed on the tires of a first-series Sd.Kfz. 222. The clearance guides (the left one also serves as a rearview mirror mount) are in their original positions, midway up the front facets of the front fenders. The license number is WH-83834. All of the driver's vision ports are fitted with removable windshield assemblies. A jack is stored on the side of the armored body, and a flagstaff is present on the front left bumper. *Holger Erdmann via Detlev Terlisten / Nuts & Bolts*

Crewmen of a first-series Sd.Kfz. 222 have decorated the antigrenade screens with flowers presented by local civilians. To the immediate rear of the left exhaust pipe is the taillight. Two of the hinged, flat-plate visors on the turret are in view; the one on the side has a vision slit, while the larger visor on the rear lacks the vision slit. *Holger Erdmann via Detlev Terlisten / Nuts & Bolts*

Two crewmen, including one with an SS emblem on his *Stahlhelm* (*left*), are scrambling into position on an Sd.Kfz. 222. This vehicle has the tall antigrenade screens and a cast-armor visor on the side of the turret. The front right fender is missing.

This early Sd.Kfz. 222 exhibits the characteristics of a first-series car. Present are the early-type flat visors and turn signals without brush guards. The left crew door is open. It has the name "Karlsbad" painted on the body.

A first-series Sd.Kfz. 222 is negotiating a steep grade. When the cannon and machine gun in the turret were elevated more than slightly, it was necessary to open the antigrenade screens. On the front left fender is the tactical sign for a reconnaissance company.

This 222, named "Danzig," helps round up stray Russian prisoners during the summer of 1941. An extra gas can has been mounted to the right rear fender. A tow cable can also be seen draped across the superstructure.

Two Sd.Kfz. 222s are on the advance. Throughout the five different series of the Sd.Kfz. 222, the front edges of the front fenders retained a straight-across design, instead of the curved design utilized on the Sd.Kfz. 221s after the earliest-production vehicles.

A first-series Sd.Kfz. 222 moves upgrade through a Belgian street in 1940. The guns are raised and the crew is alert for threats.

This Sd.Kfz. 222, license number WH-203253, has been retrofitted with a Notek blackout headlight with a brush guard on the left fender, and with brush guards for the turn signals on the sides of the armored body. With the driver's two front visors swung open, detachable windshields with wipers have been installed in the openings. The positions of the clearance guides on the front fenders are the early-production ones; later after October 1936, the guides would be moved several inches to the rear.

Two crewmen of an Sd.Kfz. 222 are conferring during winter operations. Next to the 2 cm KwK 30 cannon with a conical flash suppressor is a 7.92 mm MG 42. The MG 42 replaced the MG 13 and the MG 34 in many Sd.Kfz. 222s late in the vehicle's career.

The driver of an Sd.Kfz. 222 is peering through the open left-front visor, while the vehicle commander/gunner, *left* (with his cap and the top of his head showing), and the loader, *right*, are on watch in the turret. The antigrenade screens are equipped with canvas covers, including openings at the fronts for sighting.

The second series of the Sd.Kfz. 222 comprised seventy-two cars, with deliveries occurring in 1938. The guns of Sd.Kfz. 222 with license number WH-75972, a series 2 vehicle, are partially elevated. The range of elevation of these guns was –7 degrees to +80 degrees. Traverse was 360 degrees. The clearance guides on the front bumpers are in the later positions, at the bend between the front and the top of the bumper. *Holger Erdmann via Detlev Terlisten / Nuts & Bolts*

This vehicle, laden with a large box on the front bumper and a smaller box on the rear fender, appears to be a first-series or a second-series Sd.Kfz. 222, judging by the flat-plate visors. The storage box wedged into the front of the rear fender is a late-production item that apparently was retrofitted to this car. The jack is stored on the body next to the driver's compartment. Canvas covers are on the antigrenade screens. Near the front of the left front fender is a bracket for mounting a Notek blackout headlight.

Waffen-SS troops are clustered on an Sd.Kfz. 222, license number SS-89633, somewhere on the eastern front. The sword insignia on the front of the car was that of the 8th SS Cavalry Division, "Florian Geyer." The flat visors mark this as a first- or second-series Sd.Kfz. 222.

A feature that distinguished the third-series Sd.Kfz. 222s from the preceding series was the shroud that enclosed the rear of the armored body, replacing the original louvered door at the rear of the engine compartment. *Holger Erdmann via Detlev Terlisten / Nuts & Bolts*

This third-series Sd.Kfz. 222 of *Aufklärungs-Abteilung* 3 passes in review before Erwin Rommel and the Italian governor of Libya, General Italo Gariboldi, in Tripoli in February 1941.

"Reichenberg" is painted on the side of a fourth-series Sd.Kfz. 222 of the *Kradschützen-Lehr* Battalion. The vehicle has the tall antigrenade screen, with canvas covers on it, and the small, round wheel-hub guards. A portable fire extinguisher is on the front of the rear fender. For good luck, a horseshoe has been affixed to the side of the driver's compartment. *Holger Erdmann via Detlev Terlisten / Nuts & Bolts*

This disabled Sd.Kfz. 222 is a fourth-series car, license number WH 607863, featuring small wheel-hub guards and tall antigrenade screens. The weapons have been removed from their mounts in the turret. As a modification, storage racks have been installed on the fenders.

Some Sd.Kfz. 222s employed in North Africa were equipped with an engine-air prefilter on each side of the vehicle, to the rear of the turret. On this car, a prefilter is the canister-shaped object underneath the baggage aft of the turret. The prefilter helped eliminate some of the dust from the airstream before it entered the air cleaners and, ultimately, the carburetor.

Sd.Kfz. 222, license number WH-816165, was a fourth-series car, judging by the round wheel-hub guards, the tall antigrenade screens, and the cast-armor visors.

This vehicle was the result of a late 1940 contract for Horch to modify twenty-two light armored cars for service in the North African deserts. For twenty of the vehicles, Horch secured new fourth-series chassis, upon which the factory installed older armored bodies and turrets. Hence, this vehicle exhibits the small, round guards for the wheel hubs, a fourth-series feature, along with first-series qualities, such as the flat-plate visors and the placement of the clearance guides on the front sections of the front fenders. Add-ons that came into production after the first-series cars include the Notek blackout headlight, brush guards for that headlight and the turn signal, and the extra stowage box between the rear fender and the original storage box. *Holger Erdmann via Detlev Terlisten / Nuts & Bolts*

Crewmen of a fourth-series Sd.Kfz. 222 take a break. A *Stahlhelm* is hanging from the driver's side port. Some of the brush guard for the Notek blackout headlight is visible, with its cross-shaped brace on its left side.

An Sd.Kfz. 222 is negotiating deep sand next to a structure with a thatched roof. This is not in the North African desert, but rather at Pustynia Bledowska (Bledow Desert), in Poland, where the Wehrmacht sometimes conducted exercises. The vehicle exhibits some characteristics of the fourth series, particularly the presence of a visor on the turret below the arm of the crewman on the left. However, the location of the jack (the crank handle is visible) and the fire extinguisher on the right rear fender was a fifth-series change. A radio antenna was mounted on the top rear of the turret.

Personnel on an Sd.Kfz. 222, license number SS 49737, are keeping a watch on the horizon. This example has the tall antigrenade screen over the turret, the small wheel-hub guards, and a cast-armor visor on the side of the turret. A jerry can is hanging from the side of the body.

The same Waffen-SS Sd.Kfz. 222 is seen from the left side. The name "Alfred Szepaniak" is painted on the side of the armored body but is faintly visible, and the tactical symbol for armored car is on the side door of the engine compartment.

This captured fourth-series Sd.Kfz. 222 with the guns removed has a 6-foot reference stick lying on the ground next to it. At the rear of the car is an armored fairing that was introduced to the series during the mid-production run. The antigrenade screens on Sd.Kfz. 222 turrets were issued in high and low versions; the screens on this vehicle are of the higher type. *Patton Museum*

An Sd.Kfz. 222 is suspended from the crane of a transport ship. The outline of a tall antigrenade screen is evident under the canvas cover; the tall screen was a characteristic of the fourth series and early fifth-series Sd.Kfz. 222s. An air prefilter, for use in tropical and desert environments, is mounted on the side of the body to the rear of the turret.

Several identification features of the fifth series of the Sd.Kfz. 222 are present in this photograph. The turn signals were moved from the sides of the body to the tops of the front fenders. A storage box with two compartments and doors was added to the bottom of the existing storage boxes on the left side of the body, and a wedge-shaped box was placed between the rear fender and the storage boxes. During the latter part of fifth-series production, the visors were deleted from the sides of the turret. Finally, beginning in May 1942 production, fifth-series cars had a standard three-piece armored body, with the joint for the rear section located slightly to the front of the engine-compartment doors; this is faintly visible in this photo. *Holger Erdmann via Detlev Terlisten / Nuts & Bolts*

A soldier wearing a tropical helmet stands guard to the left as crewmen remove the 2 cm gun from the turret of an Sd.Kfz. 222. This car is from midway through the fifth-series production, since cast-armor visors are present on the turret, and the box between the original storage boxes and the rear fender, introduced in late 1942, is present. Smoke sprayers are on a rack on the front of the car. A jerry can is stored on its side in a rack on the rear part of the armored body.

A crewman of an Sd.Kfz. 222 is cleaning the barrel of the 2 cm KwK 38 cannon. A close-up view is provided of the left antigrenade screen.

Crewmen of the same Sd.Kfz. 222 are disassembling and cleaning the vehicle's MG 34 and 2 cm cannon. The turn signals are present in their late-production locations on the front fenders. The rearview mirror had been moved from its position on the left clearance guide to the top of the left turn signal.

Two of the same crewmen in the preceding photo are loading 2 cm ammunition into magazines, to the right rear of a fifth-series Sd.Kfz. 222, license number WH 1227950. The seam between the rear section of the armored body and the center section is visible to the front (*in the photo, to the right*) of the engine-compartment side door. A jack is stored on top of the rear fender.

Operating next to a wrecked house with a thatched roof, an Sd.Kfz. 222 displays a late series 5 arrangement of storage boxes on the left side of the body, as well as a turret devoid of side visors, another feature of later series 5 vehicles. The "wheel" tactical sign for a motorcycle platoon is on the side and the front of the vehicle.

Crews of two Sd.Kfz. 222 light armored cars and, in the background, an Sd.Kfz. 231 are firing their guns. The only visible marking on the cars is a white *Balkenkreuz* on the side of each one. The two Sd.Kfz. 222s have the storage box arrangements of later fifth-series vehicles.

Highlighted in the low sun, fine details are visible in this photo of a fifth-series Sd.Kfz. 222 with the tactical sign for a motorcycle platoon on the left rear fender and, faintly visible on the right rear fender, the symbol of the 10th Panzer Division. Racks for four jerry cans are in view.

The three crewmen of an Sd.Kfz. 222 are taking a break. Details in view include the cast-armor visors and the rain gutters over them, the antigrenade screens on the turret, and the barrels of the 2 cm KwK 38 cannon and the 7.92 mm MG 34.

This fifth-series Sd.Kfz. 222 was photographed patrolling the streets of Rome in September 1943. Camouflage netting is draped over the front as well as the rear of the vehicle. *BA 304-0634-28A*

A fifth-series Sd.Kfz. 222 is parked in a field near a windmill. A small, armored shield was present on the 2 cm gun mount. Next to the right elbow of the crewman to the right are the left turn signal and the rearview mirror.

The Jacques Littlefield Collection of the American Heritage Museum, in Hudson, Massachusetts, holds one of the very few surviving Sd.Kfz. 222s. It is a fifth-series example produced in 1942 and was captured by the British in North Africa in May 1943. The vehicle was restored as much as possible between 1999 and 2001. *Chris Hughes*

The Littlefield Sd.Kfz. 222 is seen from the left front. The chassis number of this vehicle is 8110148, which corresponds to the 145th vehicle of the 550 fifth-series Sd.Kfz. 222s produced. The fifth-series vehicles were designated the Sd.Kfz. 222 Ausf. B, while the first through fourth series of these light armored cars were designated Ausf. A. *Chris Hughes*

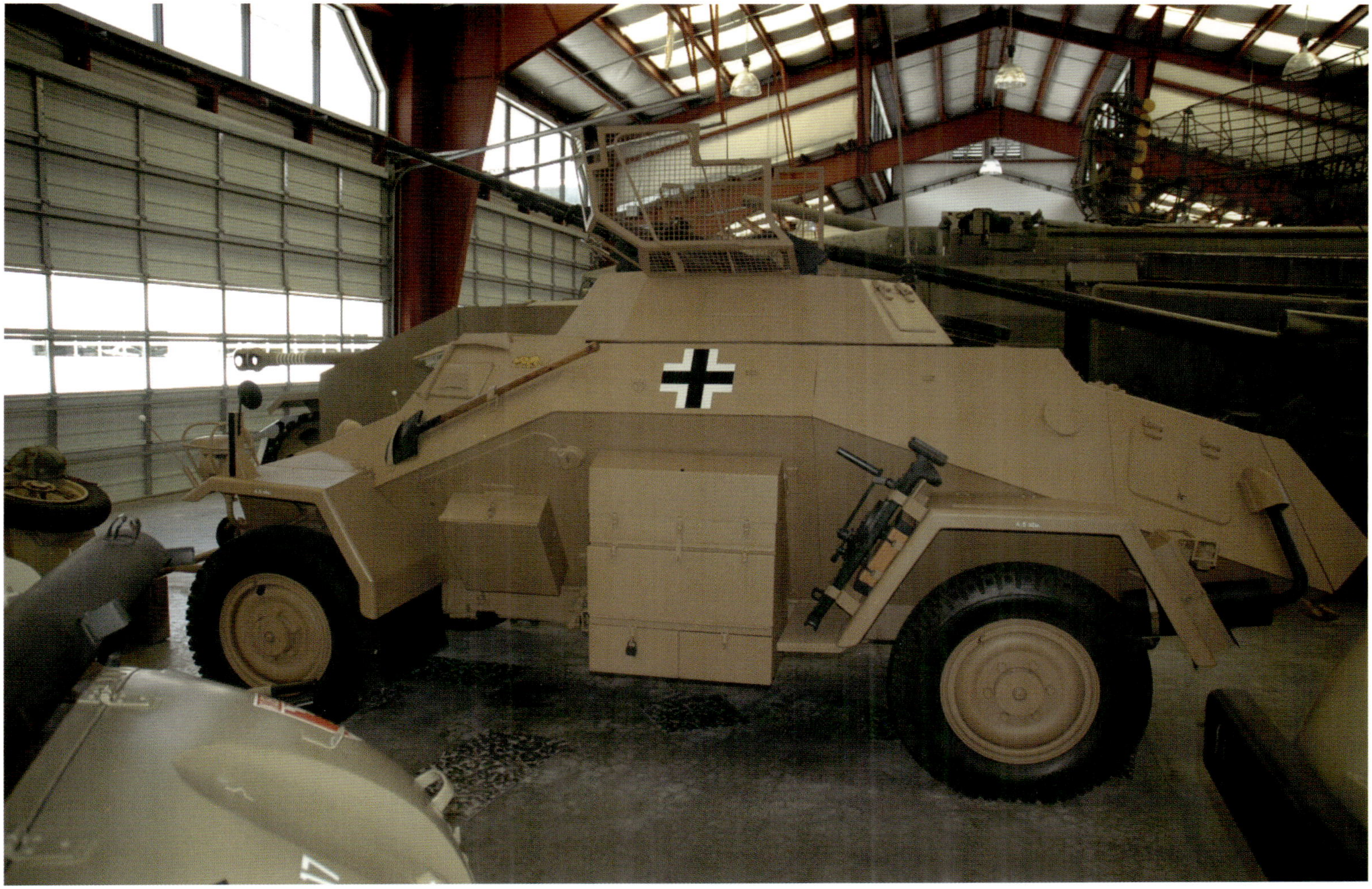

In a left-side view of the vehicle, the two vertical seams that divided the three sections of the fifth-series bodies are visible, between the storage boxes and the rear fender, and above the rear bend of the rear fender, slightly forward of the side door of the engine compartment. *Chris Hughes*

The driver's side visor and part of the front left visor are shown. Inside the side visor is the holder for a laminated glass block, which protected the driver's eyes from splinters when viewing through the vision slit. The rain gutters for the visors were fabricated from bent sheet metal and were spot-welded in place.

As seen on the front left wheel, the guard for the wheel hub was attached with three hex screws, while the wheel was mounted with eight hex lug nuts. A hole in the rim accommodates the inner tube valve.

A curved bracket and a latch secure the shovel to the side of the armored body. At the bottom is the open door for accessing the driver's compartment. The tube stored on the door held the extension hose for the driver's gas mask. The filter cartridge of the gas mask, if connected to the mask, prevented the driver from getting close enough to the vision slits. The hose got around this problem by allowing the driver to place the filter cartridge out of the way.

The storage boxes on the left side of the vehicle include a small one on the door and a large one on the armored body. The lower tier of the large box was a new feature starting with the fifth series. Padlocks are affixed to the latches.

A jack, with a wooden jack block sandwiched behind it, is stored in brackets on the front of the left rear fender. The strip on the top of the fender is a nonslip aid. The small white stencil on the side of the top of the fender is the recommended tire pressure, 4.5 Atü, the abbreviation for *Atmosphärenüberdruck*, or standard atmosphere, a way of indicating air pressure.

The left rear wheel and tire are shown close-up. The cutout for the inner tube valve on this example is different from the one on the right front wheel.

Mounted on a storage box on the left rear fender are the left license plate and a Notek convoy blackout taillight with a brush guard with a diamond-tread step on its top. A round reflector is on a metal holder below the license plate. The round plate on the side of the armored body and a corresponding plate on the opposite side covered openings where the rear legs of a frame antenna were installed when these bodies were used for fifth-series Sd.Kfz. 223 radio cars.

A closer view is provided of the left license plate, the Notek convoy light and its brush guard, and the reflector. To the lower right is the left muffler.

The armored shroud on the rear of the vehicle has a large opening on the bottom, for ventilation of the engine compartment. The two wide, rectangular openings on the plate below the bottom of the shroud were an exclusive feature of the fifth-series cars. *Chris Hughes*

In a view of the left rear suspension from the rear, at the top left is the left muffler, with the exhaust outlet on its bottom. Below the muffler is the rear coil spring; out of view is an identical coil spring to the front of the rear one. Below the spring is the lower suspension arm.

The latch socket on the right-side engine compartment door is in view. Mounted on the storage box on the right rear fender are the right license plate and, above it, a taillight with brush guard. Toward the left are the muffler and exhaust pipe, and the right-rear tow hook.

As seen in a right-rear view of the Littlefield fifth-series Sd.Kfz. 222, the engine compartment doors and the armored shroud on the rear of the body had latches that had a square socket that accepted a locking/unlocking wrench. The latch socket on the shroud is near its top, while the one on the engine compartment doors are near their lower centers.

The seam between the rear (*left*) and center (*right*) sections of the three-piece body of the fifth-series Sd.Kfz. 222s is clearly seen, between the side door of the engine compartment and the round plate.

On the deck to the rear of the turret is a grille, opening below into the rear of the fighting compartment, and a flat, trapezoidal plate. On that plate is the cover, with a swiveling handle, for the radiator filler.

As seen from the rear of the turret, the antigrenade screens are open and the 2 cm KwK 38 cannon and the 7.92 mm MG 34 are partially elevated. The curved fitting to the right of the receiver of the KwK 38 is the spent-casing deflector. In the foreground to the right of center is the radio antenna and its base.

The gun mount in the Littlefield Sd.Kfz. 222 is the 2 cm *Sockellafette* 38. The vehicle commander sat on the left side of the mount, and the loader was on the right side. The handwheel controlled both the guns' traverse and elevation. At the center is the 2 cm KwK 38 cannon. To the immediate left of the receiver of the cannon is the counterbalance mechanism, to the front of which is a 20 mm ammunition magazine, inserted in the cannon. The tan tube above the handwheel is a telescopic sight, to the right of which is the mount for a *Fliegervisier* 38 antiaircraft gunsight.

The turret is seen from the right rear. An operating arm from the 2 cm *Sockellafette* 38 to the inside of the front of the turret acted to traverse the turret in sync with the gun mount. To the left of the rear part of the 2 cm gun is the counterbalance mechanism, which made it easier for the gunner to elevate and depress the guns.

Details of the left antigrenade screen and the MG 34 are depicted. This is the "tall" screen that was used in conjunction with the 2 cm *Sockellafette* 38. Its increased height was necessary to clear the *Fliegervisier* 38 antiaircraft gunsight. The diagonal rod is a brace.

In the foreground is a mechanism on the left side of the 2 cm *Sockellafette* 38, to the front of which are the receiver of the MG 34 (*left*) and the ammunition magazine inserted in the 2 cm cannon's receiver.

Looking from the turret down into the rear of the fighting compartment, to the right is part of the 2 cm *Sockellafette* 38, and at the center are the commander's seat and diamond-tread footrest. To the left is the ventilation grille with a canvas cover, on the rear bulkhead of the compartment.

Part of the left wall of the fighting compartment is viewed from alongside the 2 cm *Sockellafette* 38 (*right*). At the center are stick grenades stored on holders. Toward the upper left is a case labeled "M.G. Werkzeug," or machine gun tools. On the box to the lower left is a *Stahlhelm* and a 2 cm ammunition magazine.

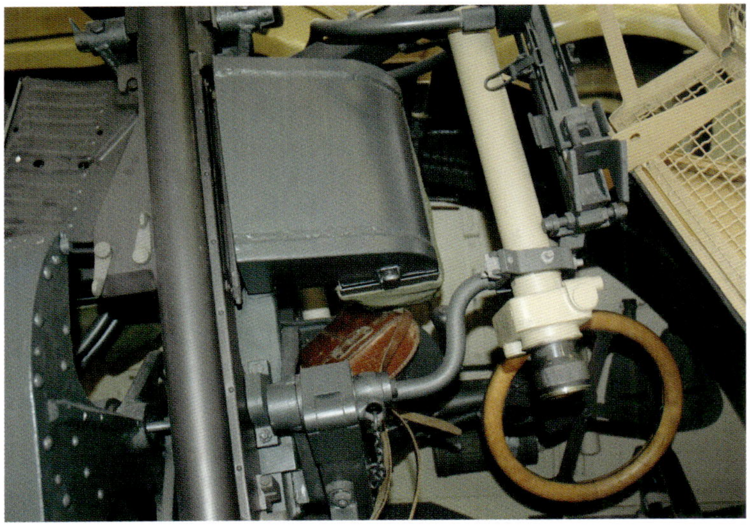

Looking down toward the gunner's station in the turret are the upper part of the weapons counterbalance (*lower left*), 2 cm magazine (*upper left*), control wheel (*lower right*), and telescopic sight and antiaircraft gunsight mount. At the center are the 2 cm KwK 38 and the spent-casings deflector.

With the turret traversed to the left, a view down into the turret includes the gunner's seat and control wheel in the foreground. Farther down and forward is the driver's compartment, with the seat back visible. The dark-yellow object in the driver's compartment is a hand grenade case.

This is a view upward and to the rear into the turret. Dominating the view is the 2 cm *Sockellafette* 38, including the handwheel for controlling elevation and traverse. The wheel is mounted on a gearbox. The lever with the knob to the right of the gearbox is a clutch lever. At the lower right is the grille on the rear of the fighting compartment.

The shield of the turret is seen from its right front, with the antigrenade grilles open and the guns elevated. On the shield toward the left is the vision slot and cover for the telescopic gunsight, the sand-colored tube to the right above the turret. A small armor shield is affixed to the 2 cm KwK 38 cannon, to fill the gap between the gun and the turret shield when the cannon is lowered.

Details of the right antigrenade screen are displayed. Two hinges secure the assembly to the turret. A nonoriginal patch made of steel was fastened over the opening for the visor on each side of the turret.

The Littlefield Sd.Kfz. 222 is observed from the right side. Visible here is the fact that the forward part of the roof of the driver's compartment was several inches higher than the roof to the rear of it. *Chris Hughes*

The fifth-series Sd.Kfz. 222, or Sd.Kfz. 222 Ausf. B, is seen from the front. The driver's visor, shown open, was considerably wider than the visor on the right front of the driver's compartment. Below the left service headlight is the horn, manufactured by Bosch. *Chris Hughes*

The Littlefield Sd.Kfz. 222 is seen from the front with both forward visors of the driver's compartment closed. The visors were made of cast armor and have vision slits near their bottoms. By design, the right front visor had a conical-head screw near each corner, while the other visors lacked those screws.

In a view from above the right front fender, the higher front portion of the driver's compartment roof is evident. The higher roof was introduced with the third series of the Sd.Kfz. 222, and it had the benefit of acting as a splash guard to protect the base of the turret shield from projectiles. Splash guards in the shape of angle irons were screwed to the roof to further protect the turret.

A storage box is recessed into each of the front fenders. The right one is seen from above. The trapezoidal lids for the boxes have a piano hinge on the front edge and a latch on the rear. Also on the fender is the right turn signal.

The front end of the Sd.Kfz. 222 is seen from the left side, showing the bumper, the horn, the left tow hook, and the left curved service headlight support. To the rear of that support is the fender support, which also forms a storage box. Below the tow hook is an armor plate with a brace on each side.

On the left fender is a Notek blackout headlight with its brush guard, along with the left turn signal and the rearview mirror. On fifth-series cars, the clearance guides were moved from their former locations, now occupied by the turn signals, to near the front outboard corners of the fenders.

The left service headlight, the Notek blackout headlight and its brush guard, the left clearance guide, and the turn signal and rearview mirror are observed from the front. Also evident is the lid of the storage box in the fender, with a piano hinge on the front edge.

Looking from between the front left tire and the front end of the armored body, elements of the front left suspension and drive mechanism are in view. Each independent suspension unit had two coil springs; the fifth-series cars had a shock absorber inside each spring. Between the front spring and the faintly visible rear spring is the drive axle, with a universal joint.

The underside of the vehicle is seen from the front, with the differential at the center and the lower suspension arms to each side of the differential. The tube to the upper right is the drag link for the front steering system. The Sd.Kfz. 222s were all-wheel-drive vehicles with independent suspensions.

The front left suspension is viewed from a close perspective, with the coil springs, enclosing shock absorbers, seated on the lower suspension arm. The tops of the springs and the shock absorbers are attached to brackets attached to the chassis frame. Between the springs is the drive axle with a universal joint. Toward the right, close to the inside of the wheel, is the steering knuckle.

Stored on the inside of the driver's door are a tube for a gas mask hose and a Wehrmacht bread bag. The door's interior side is equipped with a grab handle and a latch mechanism. On the side of the chassis fame are cables and a crank related to the brake system.

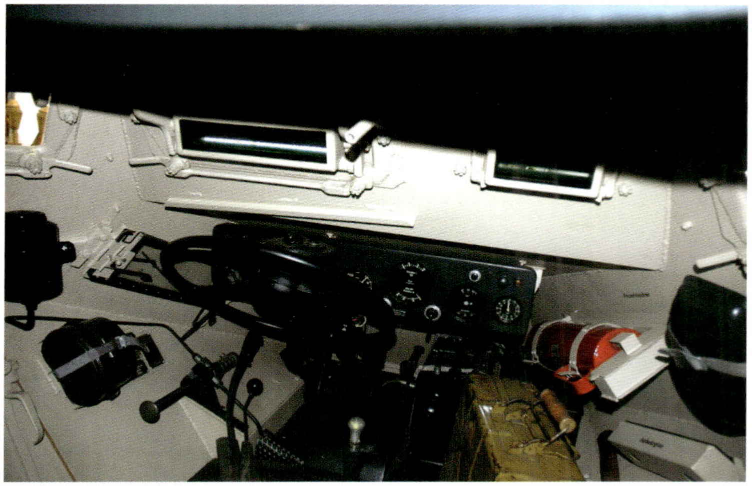

The cramped driver's compartment is observed, with the two front vision ports and visors toward the top, and steering wheel and instrument panel near the center. To the left of the steering wheel is the detachable windshield for the left front vision port. Below the windshield are a stored mess kit and the pump for the central lubrication system, and to the far left is the refill tank for the lubrication system. The battery is below the right side of the instrument panel. To the right are a hand grenade case, a fire extinguisher, a stored Notek blackout headlight, and a rack for a glass vision block.

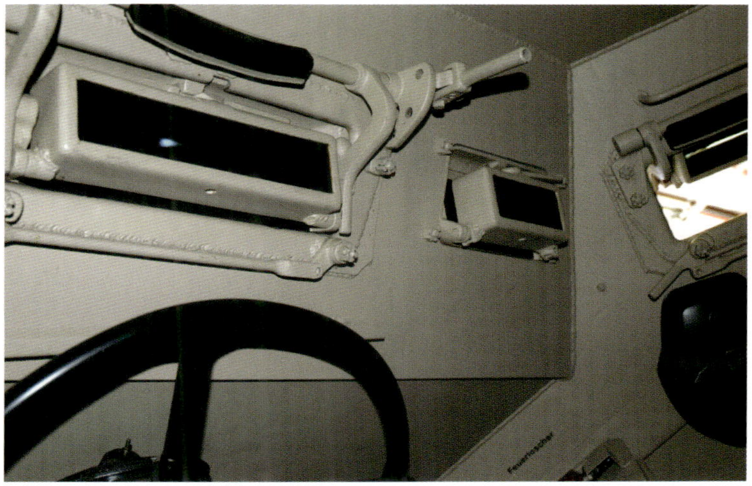

The inner sides of the two front visors, in their closed positions, and the open right-side visor (*far right*) are in view. The driver's visor was equipped with a head cushion, since it was necessary for the driver to press his eyes close to the glass vision block on the visor when viewing through the vision slit. To the right of the cushion is the operating lever for the visor.

This is a driver's-eye view of the tilted steering wheel and the instrument panel. To the lower left is the detachable windshield assembly.

Pedals to the front of the steering column are, *left to right*, clutch, brake, and accelerator. To the right is the battery, with light-colored retainer straps. To the left is the handbrake lever.

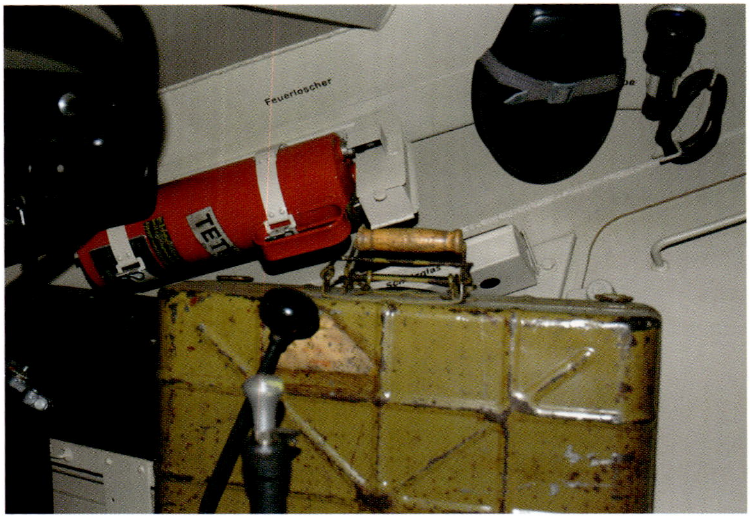

Facing to the right from the driver's seat, in the foreground are the lever for engaging all-wheel drive (with a bare-metal top) and the gearshift lever (with a black knob). Stored to the upper right are a Notek blackout headlight and a hand lamp and cord.

More of the right side of the driver's compartment is shown. At the upper left, the side visor is open; below the opening is the latching mechanism for the visor, while at the upper right corner of the opening is the operating handle. A bread bag is hung on the door (*lower center*). Above the door is a gas mask container.

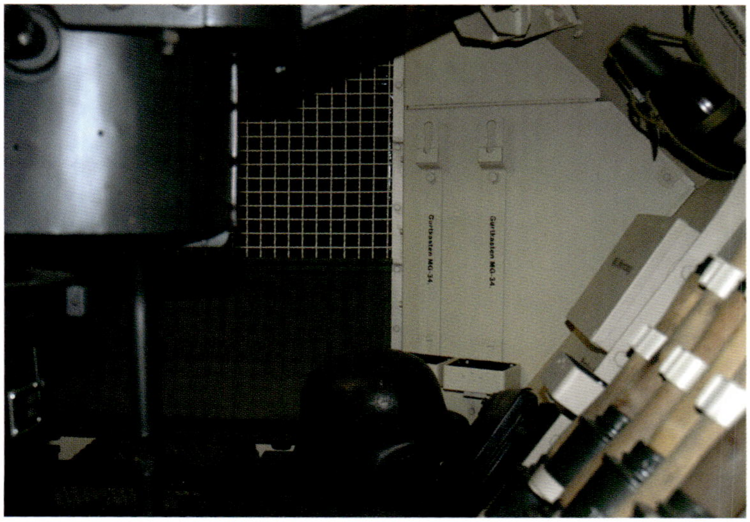

The left rear part of the fighting compartment is seen from behind the driver's seat. To the lower right, stick grenades are stored on clips. At the upper right is a canteen. To the right of the ventilation grill are two holders for 7.92 mm ammunition containers. To the upper left is part of the gun mount.

More of the left interior of the fighting compartment is shown, with the open left-side door to the lower right. In the foreground are three holders for 7.92 mm ammunition and, *at bottom*, a gas mask container. The white tube at the top center is for a gas mask tube; it is mounted on the side of the turret traversing arm, which transferred the traversing power of the gun mount to the turret shield.

The Littlefield Sd.Kfz. 222 Ausf. B is observed from the upper left rear in its museum setting. The white of the interior of the fighting compartment is visible through the ventilation grille to the rear of the turret. *Chris Hughes*

CHAPTER 3

Sd.Kfz. 223: The Communications Variant

Built upon the same specially engineered Horch 801 and 801v chassis as the Sd.Kfz. 221 and 222, the Sd.Kfz. 223 also featured four-wheel drive and four-wheel steering. Slightly heavier than the Sd.Kfz. 221 due to additional radio equipment and an extra crew member, the 223 utilized the same Horch 801 V-8 engine, resulting in somewhat reduced performance. The distinguishing characteristics separating this vehicle from the Sd.Kfz. 221 were its communications equipment and dedicated radio operator.

The Sd.Kfz. 223 operated with a three-man crew: driver, radio operator, and commander/gunner.

Like the Sd.Kfz. 221, the 223 featured a manually rotated open-topped gun shield on its roof, resembling a turret. Folding screens provided additional protection against hand grenades. Early vehicles were equipped with the MG 13, but from March 10, 1938, onward, the MG 34 became standard armament.

Production totaled 535 vehicles divided into four manufacturing groups.

Series 1 (1935–1937)

The initial production run of the Sd.Kfz. 223 comprised 117 vehicles built between 1935 and 1937. These vehicles were assembled by three manufacturers: Daimler-Benz (twelve units), Deutsche-Werke (sixty-four units), and Schichau (forty-one units). They utilized chassis numbers within the range of 810001–810359. These early models were built on the standard Horch 801 chassis and powered by a 75 hp Horch V-8 engine. Early production vehicles were armed with the MG 13 machine gun, though later ones in this series, after March 1938, would receive the MG 34. Communication equipment consisted of the 30-watt Fu 10 radio. These vehicles were designated as Ausf. A variants and featured the standard transmission, braking system, and suspension setup.

Visually, the first three series of the Sd.Kfz. 223 feature Reuleaux triangle bolt-on *Radpanzer* (armor for wheel hubs). The first series vehicles have a flagstaff on the left front fender and turn signals mounted on the sides of the body. The visors in the hull and turret were made of flat plate.

Photographed in 1935 was this trial version of the *leichter Panzerspähwagen* (Fu), or Sd.Kfz. 223. It was similar in appearance to the production first-series Sd.Kfz. 223 but lacked a gun shield. An MG 13 is installed in the opening for the turret. *Holger Erdmann via Detlev Terlisten / Nuts & Bolts*

Series 2
There were no Sd.Kfz. 223 vehicles produced with the second-series *Leichter Panzerspähwagen* (light armored car) characteristics.

Series 3 (June 1939–September 1940)
The second production batch consisted of 118 vehicles with third-series characteristics that were manufactured between June 1939 and September 1940. All vehicles in this series were assembled by MNH in Hannover and used chassis numbers between 810700 and 810817. Still designated as Ausf. A variants, these vehicles continued to use the Horch 801 chassis with the 75 hp engine. The MG 34 remained the standard armament. A change occurred in the radio equipment, with these vehicles receiving the SE 30 radio sets. Mechanically, they remained consistent with earlier versions, maintaining the standard transmission, suspension, and braking systems.

Third-series vehicles can be distinguished from their predecessors as a result of cast-armor vision slits and ports, rather than the previously used flat plate. The roof over the driver was raised compared to earlier models, providing additional headroom. The hinges for the motor hatch were now armored and no longer were of a triangular shape. A flagstaff no longer was mounted on the left front fender, where also a 35-watt Notek blackout driving light was now installed.

Series 4 (September 1940–December 1941)
The fourth series comprised 112 vehicles built by MNH in Hannover between September 1940 and December 1941. These vehicles used chassis numbers ranging from 810818 to 810414. Still classified as Ausf. A variants, they continued to utilize the Horch 801 chassis, powered by the 75 hp Horch V-8 engine. The MG 34 remained the standard armament, and they carried the SE 30 radio equipment. While minor improvements may have been incorporated on the basis of field experience, the fundamental mechanical configuration remained unchanged from the previous series.

The Reuleaux triangle bolt-on *Radpanzer* (armor for wheel hubs) used on previous models was replaced by disc-shaped hub armor.

Series 5 (July 1942–February 1944)
The fifth and final series represented a significant upgrade with the introduction of the Ausf. B variant. A total of 208 vehicles were produced between July 1942 and February 1944, with Wegman manufacturing 72 units and Weserhütte producing 136. These vehicles used chassis numbers in the range of 8110004–8110994. The most substantial change was the implementation of the improved Horch 801v chassis, which featured a more powerful 90 hp Horch V-8 engine. Also changed was the armored body, which previously was divided into two sections, was now of a standardized type consisting of three sections, and was used across multiple light armored car types. Additional enhancements included an improved transmission, power brakes, and upgraded shock absorbers for better performance in challenging terrain. Communication capabilities were significantly enhanced with the installation of the more powerful 80-watt Fu 12 radio equipment. The frame antenna was also strengthened and improved on the basis of field experience. The MG 34 remained the standard armament.

With the introduction of the fifth series, the turn signals were relocated from the sides of the armored body to the front fenders.

All Sd.Kfz. 223 vehicles produced from 1935 through February 1944 included radio equipment. The Ausf. A vehicles carried 30-watt Fu 10 or SE 30 radios, while Ausf. B vehicles featured factory-installed 80-watt Fu 12 sets. These more-powerful communication systems were also retrofitted to older Sd.Kfz. 223 vehicles.

The Sd.Kfz. 223 proved crucial in reconnaissance operations, allowing forward units to maintain contact with divisional headquarters. Bundesarchiv records show that Panzer divisions

As seen in a photo of a first-series Sd.Kfz. 223, license number WH 53806, in the field, the frame antenna was designed to swivel down and to the rear, for travel or when not in use. The rotating gun shield has flat-plate visors and slightly bowed antigrenade screens. In the well between the rear fender and the storage boxes are a fire extinguisher and a jack. *Holger Erdmann via Detlev Terlisten / Nuts & Bolts*

typically allocated these vehicles to the headquarters elements of reconnaissance battalions. The improved radio range of the Fu 12 equipment became particularly valuable on the eastern front, where units often operated beyond the range of earlier communication systems.

The distinctive frame antenna made these vehicles easily identifiable targets, leading to field modifications where crews would often remove the antenna when not in use. This practice, while reducing the vehicle's visual signature, sometimes led to damage to the delicate antenna components.

Original German maintenance records from the Wehrtechnische Studiensammlung indicate that the radio equipment in these vehicles required more-frequent maintenance than the mechanical components, particularly in extreme weather conditions. Despite these challenges, the Sd.Kfz. 223 remained an essential command and control asset throughout the war.

Three first-series Sd.Kfz. 223s are parked with antennas lowered and visors closed. On the bows of the first two cars is the insignia of *Panzer-Nachrichten-Abteilung* 38, a communications battalion serving with the 2nd Panzer Division. The lead vehicle has license plate number WH-53805, while the second car has license WH-53807. *Holger Erdmann via Detlev Terlisten / Nuts & Bolts*

Two first-series Sd.Kfz. 223s were photographed in a motor park with camouflage covers over their turrets. On the left fenders are flagstaffs, which were later discontinued. Shovels are stored on the sides of the driver's compartments.

A first-series Sd.Kfz. 223 sits alongside a Sd.Kfz. 231 (6-Rad) (*left*) and Sd.Kfz. 232 (8-Rad) along a river, probably in Poland. The *Balkenkreuz* appears to be the solid-white type used in the opening stages of the invasion of Poland. The name "York" is to the front of the cross. *Warehouse Collection*

An Sd.Kfz. 223 from the first series is following cargo trucks advancing through a bombed-out village. A rubber mud flap is on the rear of the front fender but not on the rear fenders. The machine gun in the rotating gun shield is elevated and has a dustcover over it.

Wehrmacht Heer officers are conferring next to an Sd.Kfz. 223. The small, ring-shaped fixture above the hub armor on the wheel in the foreground is a protector for the valve stem of the inner tube.

An Sd.Kfz. 231 (8-Rad) followed by what appears to be a third-series Sd.Kfz. 223 light armored car pass by battlefield wreckage. The 10 mm armor plates on the *Zusatzpanzer* on the front of the eight-wheeled car, combined with the frontal hull armor, could stop up to a 20 mm projectile. Troops occasionally fitted *Zusatzpanzer* to four-wheeled armored cars, although the practice was officially forbidden due to the limitations of the chassis.

With an open-top rotating gun shield, the Sd.Kfz. 223 was plagued with crew comfort issues during the winter, especially in Russia, as were all the *leichte Panzerspahwagens*. This led to modifications to the heater beginning in September 1942. To achieve this, the route of the engine-cooling air was reversed, so that the warm air was exhausted into the crew compartment—opposite the route desired in the desert.

Brush and tree branches have been piled up next to the rear of an Sd.Kfz. 223 for camouflage purposes. The rotating gun shield is traversed to the rear, and the 7.92 mm MG 34 is equipped with a ring sight on the barrel, for antiaircraft use. The right antigrenade screen on the turret is in the open position.

Strong sunlight reveals many details on this fifth-series Sd.Kfz. 223 (or Sd.Kfz. 223 Ausf. B), license number WH 1313897. As was the case with the Sd.Kfz. 222 Ausf. B, the location of the turn signals on the front fenders was a characteristic of the fifth series. All visors were cast armor with vision slits near the bottoms. *Holger Erdmann via Detlev Terlisten / Nuts & Bolts*

The same fifth-series Sd.Kfz. 223, license number WH 1313897, is seen from the right front. The body is mud-spattered, and a wheel rim without the tire is bolted to the side of the armored body. The structures for supporting the legs of the frame antenna changed significantly with the fifth series of the Sd.Kfz. 223. Particularly, the outriggers that supported the rear legs on the Ausf A cars were angular in cross section and had square flanges that were bolted to the body. The fifth-series / Ausf. B cars had tubular outriggers in the form of inclined Vs, with round mounting flanges. *Holger Erdmann via Detlev Terlisten / Nuts & Bolts*

CHAPTER 4

Kleiner Panzerfunkwagen (Sd.Kfz. 260 and 261)

The Sd.Kfz. 260 and 261 were *kleiner Panzerfunkwagen* (small, armored radio cars) built on the Typ 801 and 801v chassis. These specialized communications vehicles featured the same four-wheel drive and four-wheel steering as other vehicles in the series but notably lacked any armament.

Unlike their armed counterparts, these vehicles were dedicated exclusively to communications functions, with the Sd.Kfz. 260 configured for ground-to-air communications and the Sd.Kfz. 261 equipped with a distinctive large frame antenna for long-range ground communications.

Neither the Sd.Kfz. 260 nor Sd.Kfz. 261 were produced with the characteristics of the 1-3 series *leichter Panzerspähwagen* (light armored car). Rather, from the Ausf. A vehicles these included the characteristics of the fourth series, including the disc hub armor and body-mounted turn signal protected by guards, while the Ausf. B. vehicles shared characteristics of the fifth-series vehicles, with turn signals mounted on the front fenders and continuing the use of the disc hub armor.

Sd.Kfz. 260 Development

Series 4 / Ausf. A (April–July 1941)

The initial production of the Sd.Kfz. 260 began relatively late compared to other light armored car variants, with the first series commencing in April 1941. This delay was largely due to production priorities focusing on combat vehicles during the early war years. The Ausf. A variant utilized the standard Horch Typ 801 chassis with its 75 hp V-8 engine, four-wheel drive, and four-wheel-steering capability. A total of thirty-six vehicles were assembled by Weserhütte between April and July 1941.

The Sd.Kfz. 260 was designed specifically for ground-to-air communications, featuring specialized radio equipment but no armament. The vehicle maintained the same basic hull design as other vehicles in the series but replaced the turret or weapon mount with specialized communications equipment, including a distinctive antenna configuration optimized for aircraft communication. The vehicle's internal layout was completely

A trial four-wheeled, armored radio car that would be standardized as the *kleiner Panzerfunkwagen* (klPzFuWg 260), or Sd.Kfz. 260, was built in 1940. As shown here, the car's body was modeled on that of the Sd.Kfz. 222. There was no turret; a raised antigrenade screen was placed over the open-topped radio compartment. A stowage box with three latches on the bottom of the lid was mounted on the front of the body. *Holger Erdmann via Detlev Terlisten / Nuts & Bolts*

The one-off trial vehicle for the Sd.Kfz. 260 is seen from the left side. The storage box on the left side of the body was of different design than that of the Sd.Kfz. 222, having a large lower door with X reinforcing stamped on it. A single antenna was mounted on the roof adjacent to the left turn signal. *Holger Erdmann via Detlev Terlisten / Nuts & Bolts*

reconfigured to accommodate radio operators and equipment rather than weapons and ammunition.

Despite their being scheduled for earlier completion, production delays pushed the delivery of these vehicles well into the war, by which time operational experience had already highlighted the need for improved mobility and reliability.

Series 5 / Ausf. B (April 1942–April 1943)

The second and more substantial production group of the Sd. Kfz. 260 featured significant improvements consistent with those implemented across the fifth series of light armored cars, most notably the implementation of the upgraded Horch Typ 801v chassis, with its more powerful 90 hp engine, improved transmission, enhanced suspension, and power brakes. A total of ninety-six Ausf. B vehicles were produced by Weserhuette from April 1942 through April 1943.

These vehicles incorporated lessons learned from early field experience, with enhanced radio equipment and improved internal layout for the communications operators. The Ausf. B variant, with its more powerful engine and upgraded chassis, offered better mobility and reliability in difficult terrain, addressing limitations observed in the earlier Ausf. A vehicles. The communication equipment was also updated to maintain compatibility with evolving Luftwaffe radio systems.

The total production of the Sd.Kfz. 260 reached 132 vehicles before production ceased in April 1943.

Sd.Kfz. 261 Development

Series 4 / Ausf. A (April 1941–March 1942)

The Sd.Kfz. 261, specialized for long-range ground communications, began production concurrently with the Sd.Kfz. 260 in April 1941. The Ausf. A series production numbers were substantially larger than its ground-to-air counterpart, with 215 vehicles produced by Weserhütte at Bad Oeynhausen between April 1941 and March 1942. These vehicles utilized the standard Horch Typ 801 chassis, with its 75 hp engine.

The most distinctive feature of the Sd.Kfz. 261 was its large frame antenna, which enabled long-range ground communications essential for coordinating widely dispersed reconnaissance elements. This large antenna structure, while providing excellent communication range, made the vehicle highly recognizable and potentially vulnerable to enemy fire. Like the Sd.Kfz. 260, the 261 carried no armament, with interior space dedicated entirely to radio operators and communications equipment.

The internal configuration included positions for additional radio operators compared to the Sd.Kfz. 260, reflecting its role in maintaining continuous communication with multiple ground units simultaneously. The communications equipment was more powerful than that in the Sd.Kfz. 260, requiring additional power systems and cooling arrangements.

Series 5 / Ausf. B (April 1942–April 1943)

The improved Ausf. B variant of the Sd.Kfz. 261 featured the same significant chassis upgrades as the Sd.Kfz. 260 Ausf. B, implementing the Horch Typ 801v chassis, with its 90 hp engine and associated mechanical improvements. Weserhuette produced 137 of these vehicles between April 1942 and April 1943.

The Ausf. B incorporated various refinements on the basis of field experience, including improved antenna-mounting systems designed to better withstand rough terrain and to allow more rapid deployment and stowage. The radio equipment was also updated to maintain compatibility with evolving Wehrmacht communication standards and to improve reliability in adverse conditions.

The total production of the Sd.Kfz. 261 reached 352 vehicles before production ceased in April 1943.

The Sd.Kfz. 261 shared the same body and chassis as the Sd.Kfz. 260 but had long-range, ground-to-ground radio equipment as well as a frame antenna. Shown here is a trial Sd.Kfz. 261, based on an Sd.Kfz. 222 and completed by the early spring of 1940. *Holger Erdmann via Detlev Terlisten / Nuts & Bolts*

Operational Use and Field Modifications

Both the Sd.Kfz. 260 and Sd.Kfz. 261 were primarily assigned to headquarters elements of reconnaissance battalions and higher-echelon units, where their specialized communication capabilities were most valuable. The Sd.Kfz. 260's ground-to-air communication capability became particularly important for coordination with Luftwaffe close-air-support aircraft, especially during the early Blitzkrieg campaigns. However, as Allied air superiority increased, these vehicles became prime targets and often operated with camouflage netting to conceal their distinctive antenna arrays.

Common field modifications to the Sd.Kfz. 260 and Sd.Kfz. 261 included the following:

- Camouflage systems: Elaborate camouflage arrangements to conceal the distinctive antenna systems, particularly for the Sd.Kfz. 261 with its large frame antenna
- Quick-detach antenna mounts: Modifications to allow more-rapid stowage of antenna systems when under air attack
- Additional power systems: Field-installed auxiliary generators to support extended communication operations without running the main engine
- Winterization kits: For eastern front operations, including additional heaters to keep sensitive radio equipment functional in extreme cold
- Enhanced grounding systems: Particularly for the Sd. Kfz. 261, to improve radio performance in varied terrain conditions

Bundesarchiv records indicate that the Sd.Kfz. 261 was particularly valued for its long-range communication capabilities. During the Russian campaign, when units frequently operated beyond normal radio range, these vehicles sometimes formed relay networks to maintain command communications across the vast eastern front.

Both vehicles remained in service until the war's end, with surviving units increasingly concentrated in the western theater as the war progressed, where they faced less severe conditions than on the eastern front.

A fourth-series Sd.Kfz. 260 sits among several of its contemporaries in a traffic jam, among them a Sd.Kfz. 250 half-track (*far left*), an eight-wheeled Sd.Kfz. 232, and a four-wheeled Sd.Kfz. 223 radio vehicle (*far right*). The scene is July 1942 in the lower Don region of the Soviet Union. The unit is the *Kradschützenbatalion* "Großdeutchland." "GD" had a squadron of armored cars, as well as *Kradschützen* in half-tracks, *Kübelwagen*, and motorcycles. Interestingly, members of the armored-car squadron wore gold-yellow branch colors on their uniforms, while the *Kradschützen* wore meadow green. *BA 101I-748-0100A-16*

The trial Sd.Kfz. 261 is observed from the left side with the frame antenna folded down. Like the Sd.Kfz. 260, the Sd.Kfz. 261 had an antigrenade screen over the opening in the roof above the radio compartment. *Holger Erdmann via Detlev Terlisten / Nuts & Bolts*

Machine gun fire chewed up the front of the body of this Wehrmacht Heer Sd.Kfz. 261 with its frame antenna deployed. A tow cable is wrapped around the tow hooks, and all the visors are open.

An Afrika Korps Sd.Kfz. 261 heavily laden with crew baggage and gear has paused during operations in the desert. A locally fabricated rack on the front of the vehicle holds four jerry cans, and an extra storage box has been secured to the front fender.

This Sd.Kfz. 261 Ausf. A is being prepared for rail movement. The screen arrangement that protected the radio compartment is raised here and can be seen to good advantage. A small generator is installed in the stowage box on the left-hand side. This was used to test the radios when the engine was shut down. The fuel hose can be seen dangling from the corner of the box. This vehicle bears the markings of a signals unit of the 5th Panzer Division. The dark areas around the insignia appear to indicate this vehicle has been repainted overall dark yellow.

This Sd.Kfz. 261 is distinguished as a fifth-series vehicle by several characteristics: the extra storage boxes under the original one on the side of the body and to the rear of the original box, and the location of the turn signals on the front fenders. A shovel is stored on the side of the driver's compartment. *Holger Erdmann via Detlev Terlisten / Nuts & Bolts*

The Sd.Kfz. 261 was equipped with the FuG 12 radio system, a medium-wave transceiver designed specifically for tank command communications. This unit offered enhanced performance compared to the FuG 10, boasting an 80-watt transmission capability. Meanwhile, the Sd.Kfz. 260 variant utilized the VHF-based FuG 7 transceiver, typically configured with a 1.4-meter antenna—making the primary visual distinction between models the distinctive frame antenna. Worth noting is that the FuG 7 was compatible with the Luftwaffe's FuG 17 transceiver, facilitating effective ground-air coordination during support operations. In this particular image, we see the vehicle as part of a larger reconnaissance unit, with its frame antenna shown in the folded position.

With both hatches of the antigrenade screen open on a fifth-series Sd.Kfz. 261, a crewman has poked his head above the screen and is looking at the photographer. Two "Liebstandarte SS Adolf Hitler" insignia are on the vehicle, to the far left and below the side visor of the driver's compartment. An SS license plate that reads either 163240 or 163940 is on the rear fender.

Waffen-SS vehicles and troops, including a fifth-series Sd.Kfz. 261 with license plate number 108818 in the foreground, are operating in a narrow lane in a woodland. Blackout covers without slots are fitted over the service headlights.

Soviet prisoners of war are on the left side of an Sd.Kfz. 261. The Wehrmacht Heer license plate is obscured, but the legible part of the number is 312612. Above the license plate, the whitewash camouflage was not applied over the divisional and tactical symbols. On the left is what appears to be the insignia of 24th Panzer Division, and to the right is the tactical sign for a signals company. A 7.92 mm MG 42 with an armored shield, likely scavenged from a half-track, has been mounted on the roof of the driver's compartment.

A mud-caked and evidently whitewashed Sd.Kfz. 261, license number WH 1820158, is preceding what appears to be an Sd.Kfz. 222 during a winter operation. A spare tire is stored atop the vehicle, and a canvas cover is over the radio compartment.

Comparison of German WWII Light Armored Cars (Sd.Kfz. 221–261 Series)					
Characteristic	**Sd.Kfz. 221 Ausf. A**	**Sd.Kfz. 222 Ausf. A**	**Sd.Kfz. 222 Ausf. B**	**Sd.Kfz. 223 Ausf. A**	**Sd.Kfz. 223 Ausf. B**
General information					
Production period	1935–1940	1937–1942	1942–1944	1937–1942	1942–1944
Role	reconnaissance	light recon / combat	light recon / combat	radio communications	radio communications
Chassis base	Horch 801	Horch 801	Horch 801	Horch 801	Horch 801
Automotive characteristics					
Engine	Horch V-8, 3.5 L	Horch V-8, 3.5 L	Horch V-8, 3.8 L	Horch V-8, 3.5 L	Horch V-8, 3.8 L
Horsepower	75 hp	75 hp	90 hp	75 hp	90 hp
Transmission	4-speed manual	4-speed manual	4-speed manual	4-speed manual	4-speed manual
Drive	4 × 4	4 × 4	4 × 4	4 × 4	4 × 4
Length	4.8 m (15 ft., 9 in.)	4.8 m (15 ft., 9 in.)	4.8 m (15 ft., 9 in.)	4.8 m (15 ft., 9 in.)	4.8 m (15 ft., 9 in.)
Width	1.95 m (6 ft., 5 in.)	1.95 m (6 ft., 5 in.)	1.95 m (6 ft., 5 in.)	1.95 m (6 ft., 5 in.)	1.95 m (6 ft., 5 in.)
Height	1.7 m (5 ft., 7 in.)	2.0 m (6 ft., 7 in.)	2.0 m (6 ft., 7 in.)	2.0 m (6 ft., 7 in.)	2.0 m (6 ft., 7 in.)
Weight	4.0 tons (8,818 lbs.)	4.3 tons (9,480 lbs.)	4.5 tons (9,920 lbs.)	4.2 tons (9,259 lbs.)	4.4 tons (9,700 lbs.)
Performance					
Maximum road speed	80 km/h (50 mph)	80 km/h (50 mph)	85 km/h (53 mph)	80 km/h (50 mph)	80 km/h (50 mph)
Cross-country speed	30 km/h (19 mph)	30 km/h (19 mph)	35 km/h (22 mph)	30 km/h (19 mph)	35 km/h (22 mph)
Range (road)	300 km (186 miles)	300 km (186 miles)	320 km (199 miles)	300 km (186 miles)	320 km (199 miles)
Fording depth	0.6 m (2 ft.)	0.6 m (2 ft.)	0.6 m (2 ft.)	0.6 m (2 ft.)	0.6 m (2 ft.)
Gradient	30°	30°	30°	30°	30°
Armament					
Main armament	MG 34 7.92 mm	2 cm KwK 30/38	2 cm KwK 38	MG 34 7.92 mm	MG 34 7.92 mm
Secondary armament	none	MG 34 7.92 mm	MG 34 7.92 mm	none	none
Ammunition	1,500 rounds 7.92 mm	180 rounds 20 mm + 1,500 rounds 7.92 mm	180 rounds 20 mm + 1,500 rounds 7.92 mm	1,000 rounds 7.92 mm	1,000 rounds 7.92 mm
Turret	open-topped	open-topped with mesh	improved open-topped with mesh	frame antenna	frame antenna
Armor protection					
Hull front	8 mm (0.31 in.)	14.5 mm (0.57 in.)	14.5 mm (0.57 in.)	14.5 mm (0.57 in.)	14.5 mm (0.57 in.)
Hull sides	8 mm (0.31 in.)	8 mm (0.31 in.)	8 mm (0.31 in.)	8 mm (0.31 in)	8 mm (0.31 in.)
Hull rear	8 mm (0.31 in.)	8 mm (0.31 in.)	8 mm (0.31 in.)	8 mm (0.31 in)	8 mm (0.31 in.)
Turret	8 mm (0.31 in.)	14.5 mm (0.57 in.)	14.5 mm (0.57 in.)	8 mm (0.31 in.)	8 mm (0.31 in.)
Radio equipment					
Short range	Fu.Sprd.a	Fu.Sprd.a	Fu.Sprd.a	Fu.Sprd.a	Fu.Sprd.a
Long range	none	none	none	Fu 12 SE 80	Fu 12 SE 80
Frame antenna	no	no	no	yes (2 m / 6.6 ft.)	yes (2 m / 6.6 ft.)

Characteristic	Sd.Kfz. 221 Ausf. A	Sd.Kfz. 222 Ausf. A	Sd.Kfz. 222 Ausf. B	Sd.Kfz. 223 Ausf. A	Sd.Kfz. 223 Ausf. B
Crew					
Total	2	3	3	3	3
Commander	yes	yes	yes	yes	yes
Driver	yes	yes	yes	yes	yes
Gunner	no	yes	yes	no	no
Radio operator	no	no	no	yes	yes
Special features					
Notable features	basic recon	enhanced turret screen for grenade protection	enhanced turret screen, improved engine	large frame antenna for communication	large frame antenna, improved engine

Characteristic	Sd.Kfz. 260 Ausf. A	Sd.Kfz. 260 Ausf. B	Sd.Kfz. 261 Ausf. A	Sd.Kfz. 261 Ausf. B
General information				
Production period	1940–1942	1942–1944	1940–1942	1942–1944
Role	radio vehicle	radio vehicle	long-range radio	long-range radio
Chassis base	Horch 801	Horch 801	Horch 801	Horch 801
Automotive characteristics				
Engine	Horch V-8, 3.5 L	Horch V-8, 3.8 L	Horch V-8, 3.5 L	Horch V-8, 3.8L
Horsepower	75 hp	90 hp	75 hp	90 hp
Transmission	4-speed manual	4-speed manual	4-speed manual	4-speed manual
Drive	4 × 4	4 × 4	4 × 4	4 × 4
Length	4.8 m (15 ft., 9 in.)	4.8 m (15 ft., 9 in.)	4.8 m (15 ft., 9 in.)	4.8 m (15 ft., 9 in.)
Width	1.95 m (6 ft., 5 in.)	1.95 m (6 ft., 5 in.)	1.95 m (6 ft., 5 in.)	1.95 m (6 ft., 5 in.)
Height	1.7 m (5 ft., 7 in.)	1.7 m (5 ft., 7 in.)	2.0 m (6 ft., 7 in.)	2.0 m (6 ft., 7 in.)
Weight	4.0 tons (8,818 lbs.)	4.2 tons (9,259 lbs.)	4.1 tons (9,039 lbs.)	4.3 tons (9,480 lbs.)
Performance				
Maximum road speed	80 km/h (50 mph)	85 km/h (53 mph)	80 km/h (50 mph)	80 km/h (50 mph)
Cross-country speed	30 km/h (19 mph)	35 km/h (22 mph)	30 km/h (19 mph)	35 km/h (22 mph)
Range (road)	300 km (186 miles)	320 km (199 miles)	300 km (186 miles)	320 km (199 miles)
Fording depth	0.6 m (2 ft.)	0.6 m (2 ft.)	0.6 m (2 ft.)	0.6 m (2 ft.)
Gradient	30°	30°	30°	30°
Armament				
Main armament	none	none	none	none
Secondary armament	none	none	none	none
Ammunition	none	none	none	none
Turret	none	none	none	none

Characteristic	Sd.Kfz. 260 Ausf. A	Sd.Kfz. 260 Ausf. B	Sd.Kfz. 261 Ausf. A	Sd.Kfz. 261 Ausf. B
Armor protection				
Hull front	8 mm (0.31 in.)	8 mm (0.31 in.)	8 mm (0.31 in.)	8 mm (0.31 in.)
Hull sides	8 mm (0.31 in.)	8 mm (0.31 in.)	8 mm (0.31 in.)	8 mm (0.31 in.)
Hull rear	8 mm (0.31 in.)	8 mm (0.31 in.)	8 mm (0.31 in.)	8 mm (0.31 in.)
Turret	N/A	N/A	N/A	N/A
Radio equipment				
Short range	Fu.Sprd.a	Fu.Sprd.a	Fu.Sprd.a	Fu.Sprd.a
Long range	Fu 12 SE 80	Fu 12 SE 80	Fu 12 SE 80 + Fu.Sprd.f	Fu 12 SE 80 + Fu.Sprd.f
Frame antenna	No	no	yes (9 m / 29.5 ft.)	yes (9 m / 29.5 ft.)
Crew				
Total	2	2	3	3
Commander	yes	yes	yes	yes
Driver	yes	yes	yes	yes
Gunner	no	no	no	no
Radio operator	no	no	yes	yes
Special features				
Notable features	radio car without armament	radio car without armament, improved engine	9 m rod antenna for long-range comms	9 m rod antenna, improved engine

Notes:
The Ausf. B variants typically featured improved engines, slightly better performance, and improved armored bodies.
The Sd.Kfz. 222 was the most heavily armed of the series with its 20 mm autocannon.
Sd.Kfz. 260/261 were dedicated radio vehicles with no offensive armament.
The frame antenna on the Sd.Kfz. 223 (2 m / 6.6 ft. height) and the rod antenna on the Sd.Kfz. 261 (9 m / 29.5 ft. height) were their most distinctive visual features.
All vehicles used the same basic Horch chassis with differing superstructures and equipment.

CHAPTER 5

S gl gep Personenkraftwagen (Sd.Kfz. 247)

The Sd.Kfz. 247, designated as *schwerer geländegängiger gepanzerter* (s gl gep) *Personenkraftwagen* (heavy cross-country armored staff car), represented a specialized command vehicle designed for armored reconnaissance units. Unlike other German light armored cars of the period, which evolved through multiple iterations of the same basic design, the Sd.Kfz. 247 existed in two distinctly different variants: a six-wheeled version and a later four-wheeled version, with both retaining the same designation due to their identical functional role.

Sd.Kfz. 247 (Sechsrad/Six-Wheeled), 1937–1938

The initial Sd.Kfz. 247 was based on the Krupp L2H143 chassis, commonly known as the "Krupp Protze" (Krupp limber), which had been specifically developed for military applications. This six-wheeled platform was already in use for various military vehicles, making it a logical choice for the armored-staff-car role. Powered by Krupp's distinctive horizontally opposed air-cooled engine, a total of ten vehicles were manufactured between 1937 and January 1938.

The six-wheeled Sd.Kfz. 247 featured an open-topped design with armor protection sufficient to withstand 7.92 mm armor-piercing rounds fired from a distance of at least 30 yards. The vehicle could carry a driver and five passengers, typically reconnaissance unit officers and staff. No provision was made for mounted armament or communications equipment, since the vehicle was intended purely as a protected transport and mobile command post.

The Krupp chassis provided good off-road mobility with its three-axle design, though its high profile and distinctive appearance made it relatively conspicuous on the battlefield. The engine was positioned in the front of the vehicle, with the crew compartment behind. The open-topped design allowed for good visibility and situational awareness, though it provided no protection from overhead threats or adverse weather conditions.

These initial six-wheeled vehicles saw limited operational use during the early campaigns in Poland and France, primarily serving with senior reconnaissance officers as intended. Their limited production numbers restricted their overall impact on operations.

Sd.Kfz. 247 (Vierrad/Four-Wheeled), 1941–1942

In 1938, the German military ordered an additional fifty-eight Sd.Kfz. 247 vehicles, but with substantial design changes. The new version would be based on the Horch *Einheitsfahrgestell* II (uniform chassis II), representing a significant departure from the earlier six-wheeled configuration.

It's important to note the German practice of assigning Sd. Kfz. numbers on the basis of a vehicle's function rather than its design. This approach differed from systems such as the US Army's Standard Nomenclature List (SNL G-numbers), which categorized vehicles primarily by their technical characteristics. As a result, despite the fundamental design differences between the six-wheeled and four-wheeled versions, both retained the Sd.Kfz. 247 designation due to their shared role as armored staff cars.

Production of the four-wheeled variant faced numerous delays and began only in July 1941. Daimler-Benz completed the contracted fifty-eight vehicles by January 1942. Unlike most other German four-wheeled armored vehicles of the period, which featured four-wheel steering, the four-wheeled Sd.Kfz. 247 was equipped with four-wheel drive but only two-wheel steering. This design choice likely simplified production and maintenance while retaining adequate mobility for its command role.

The four-wheeled Sd.Kfz. 247 maintained the same capacity as its predecessor, accommodating a driver and five passengers. It also retained the open-topped configuration and front-engine layout. As with the six-wheeled version, no provisions were made for mounted weapons or specialized communications equipment, underscoring its dedicated role as a protected transport for command personnel.

By the time these vehicles entered service in 1942, the operational environment had changed significantly. The vehicle's intended role had largely been taken over by other platforms, and as a result, the four-wheeled Sd.Kfz. 247 vehicles were primarily assigned to headquarters elements of motorcycle units rather than their originally intended role with armored reconnaissance formations.

Field Service and Modifications

The limited production numbers of both variants of the Sd.Kfz. 247 meant they never had the widespread impact of other German armored vehicles. The six-wheeled variant saw some action during the Polish and French campaigns of 1939–1940, while the four-wheeled version arrived too late for the early Blitzkrieg operations but was documented in use during Operation Barbarossa, primarily with motorcycle battalions as originally intended.

The open-topped design proved particularly problematic during winter operations on the eastern front, leading to field modifications including improvised canvas covers and winterization measures. Some vehicles received additional stowage capacity for extended operations, and there are records of attempts to install basic radio equipment in some units, though this was not a standard feature.

By 1943, most surviving vehicles had been transferred to secondary theaters or rear areas, where they served in various command and liaison roles until the end of the war.

In 1937 Daimler-Benz produced a total of ten six-wheeled armored staff cars with a front engine; it was designated the Sd.Kfz. 247 (later Sd.Kfz. 247 Ausf. A). These vehicles borrowed their chassis, engines, and suspensions from the Krupp L2H 143 Prötze truck. The driver's compartment and the personnel compartment were open-topped. *Tom Laemlein collection*

Although the leading axle of the tandem rear suspension is obscured in this view, it does provide a sense of scale for the vehicle. Flat-plate visors were provided for the crew, providing a modest degree of protection.

Introduced after the completion of the 10 Sd.Kfz. 247 Ausf A by Daimler-Benz, a second version of the Sd.Kfz. 247 was produced by Krupp, with fifty-eight examples being completed. These cars incorporated an entirely different design, with four wheels and an entirely redesigned body. The vehicle in the photograph was a trial example or prototype. It had an open top over the personnel compartment (seen here with a cover over it), long cooling louvers on the side of the engine compartment, a spare tire stored on the rear of the body, and three visors on the side of the body.

The insignia of "Liebstandarte SS Adolf Hitler" as it appeared from 1943 to the end of the war is near the rear of the armored body of an Sd.Kfz. 260 crossing tracks in a railroad yard. The rod antenna is on the rear part of the body. It was connected to a suite of radio sets collectively designated as klPzFuTr "D" (mot) set; this suite used the same frequency band as aircraft.

The second type of production Sd.Kfz. 247s featured a ventilation cowling instead of long louvers on the side of the engine compartment, cooling louvers, two separate visors on the front of the driver's compartment, double side-entry doors, muffler and exhaust pipe on the front right fender, and a raised roof over the driver's compartment. *Holger Erdmann via Detlev Terlisten / Nuts & Bolts*

Officers are conferring on and around an Sd.Kfz. 247 while a PzKpfw III stands guard in the background. The vehicle has a subtle camouflage paint application and a light-colored band on the lower part of the front fender.

In a photo of an officer of the 6th Panzer Division wearing a Knight's Cross and standing in an Sd.Kfz. 247, the raised roof over the driver's compartment is discernible under his left arm and hand. Two of the cast-armor visors with vision slits on the side of the personnel compartment are in view, as well as the right turn signal, farther forward.

At the front of a column of vehicles is an Sd.Kfz. 247 bearing license number WH 651557. Markings on the front of the vehicle include the *Stahlhelm* symbol of "Großdeutschland" and the tactical symbol for a motorcycle platoon with "St" (staff) next to it. Above the personnel compartment, a *Sternantenne* (star antenna) has been erected. To the rear of the left front fender is the open side door.

Sd.Kfz. 247 Series Comparison		
Feature	**Sd.Kfz. 247 (Sechsrad/six-wheeled)**	**Sd.Kfz. 247 (Vierrad/four-wheeled)**
Production period	1937–January 1938	July 1941–January 1942
Quantity	10	58
Manufacturer	Krupp	Daimler-Benz
Chassis type	Krupp L2H143 ("Krupp Protze")	Horch *Einheitsfahrgestell* II (uniform chassis II)
Engine	Krupp horizontally opposed air-cooled	Horch engine
Drive configuration	6 × 4 (six wheels, four driven)	4 × 4 (four-wheel drive)
Steering	front wheels	front wheels only (two-wheel steering)
Armor protection	resistant to 7.92 mm AP rounds from 30+ yards	resistant to 7.92 mm AP rounds from 30+ yards
Armament	none	none
Communications equipment	none standard	none standard
Body style	open-topped	open-topped
Engine position	front	front
Crew capacity	driver + 5 passengers	driver + 5 passengers
Original intended use	command vehicle for armored reconnaissance units	command vehicle for armored reconnaissance units
Actual field deployment	reconnaissance command during Polish and French campaigns	headquarters of motorcycle units
Distinctive features	six-wheel configuration, high profile	four-wheel configuration, simplified chassis compared to other German 4×4 armored cars
Notable limitations	conspicuous size, limited protection from overhead threats	late entry into service, limited utility in evolved combat environment

Notes:

Despite the substantial differences in design and chassis, both vehicles retained the same Sd.Kfz. 247 designation due to their identical functional role.
German practice assigned Sd.Kfz. numbers on the basis of vehicle function rather than design.
Neither variant included provisions for mounted weapons or specialized communications equipment.
Both variants maintained an open-topped design for improved visibility and command observation.
The four-wheeled variant was ordered in 1938, but production delays pushed completion to 1941–1942.
By the time the four-wheeled variant entered service, its original intended role had largely been filled by other vehicles.
Field modifications often included improvised weather protection and occasionally the addition of basic radio equipment.
The six-wheeled variant is particularly rare, with few surviving examples.